"This is a fresh, modern book on personal spirituality. So many of us are taken up with the distractions of our work, our phones, and our own inner chatter, that it is hard to find a path back to ourselves. Bonowitz shows how aspects of monastic life can help. He begins quite simply with the power of silence and sustaining solitude. From this base, one can develop other practices (meditating on a word, prayer, the focus that comes from cooking and communal work) that can still the mind and open the heart to a spirituality of deeper self-understanding."

> — Sherry Turkle, MIT professor and author of *Alone Together: Why We Expect More from Technology and Less from Each Other* and *Reclaiming Conversation: The Power of Talk in a Digital Age*

"Dom Bernardo has the rare gift for distilling decades of experience in formation work into real gems of wisdom and insight, at once deeply contemplative and eminently practical. This book is a precious gift to those seeking God with St. Benedict as their guide."

> — Gerard D'Souza
> Abbey of Genesee

"Bonowitz's book, written in a very agreeable style and with much humor, will stimulate a desire in young people to embrace the monastic life. It shows the way that a monk's experience develops over the course of a lifetime, with both its struggles and its joys. Reading it, many will discover their thirst for God, as well as their yearning to find their true self and the way to genuine freedom and life. Not only religious men and women, but lay Christians will also find new impetus to live out their vocation."

"As a Benedictine nun who has profited from the works of Cistercian authors, I would say, 'Take up and read!'"

> — Sister Teresa Paula Perdigão, OSB
> Mosteiro do Encontro, Paraná, Brazil

"How does the Christian reach those lofty summits of love to which St. Benedict directs us in his Rule? In this book we listen in to the guidance Abbot Bernard Bonowitz has given his own novices. He offers sound, realistic, and compassionate advice of a spiritual father delivered with love and a touch of humor. He never takes his eye off the goal, but outlining the essentials of monastic spirituality, gently leads every novice-Christian out of self, towards others and into communion with God. This is a rich handbook on spiritual growth."

> — Father Brendan Thomas, Belmont Abbey, UK

D1452020

MONASTIC WISDOM SERIES: NUMBER SIXTY-TWO

Truly Seeking God

Bernard Bonowitz, OCSO

α

Cistercian Publications
www.cistercianpublications.org

LITURGICAL PRESS
Collegeville, Minnesota
www.litpress.org

A Cistercian Publications title published by Liturgical Press

Cistercian Publications
Editorial Offices
161 Grosvenor Street
Athens, Ohio 45701
www.cistercianpublications.org

Scripture texts in this work are translated by Fr. Bernard Bonowitz.

© 2019 by Bernard Bonowitz
Published by Liturgical Press, Collegeville, Minnesota. All rights reserved.
No part of this book may be used or reproduced in any manner whatsoever,
except brief quotations in reviews, without written permission of Liturgical
Press, Saint John's Abbey, PO Box 7500, Collegeville, MN 56321-7500. Printed
in the United States of America.

1   2   3   4   5   6   7   8   9

Library of Congress Cataloging-in-Publication Data

Names: Bonowitz, Bernard, author.
Title: Truly seeking God / Bernard Bonowitz, OCSO.
Description: Collegeville : Cistercian Publications, 2019. | Series: Monastic
    wisdom series ; NUMBER 62 | Summary: "Recounts the ways in which
    monks actively seek God in all the practices and places of the monastic
    life and describes the gradual growth and transformation from novice
    to young solemnly professed to elder monk"—Provided by publisher.
Identifiers: LCCN 2019020919 (print) | ISBN 9780879072629 (pbk.)
Subjects: LCSH: Monastic and religious life. | Monasticism and religious
    orders. | Spiritual life—Christianity.
Classification: LCC BX2435 .B674 2019 (print) | LCC BX2435 (ebook) |
    DDC 255—dc23
LC record available at https://lccn.loc.gov/2019020919
LC ebook record available at https://lccn.loc.gov/2019981486

Contents

The Making of a Monk

Introduction

During the greater part of the second millennium—from the beginning of the thirteenth century until the Second Vatican Council in the middle of the twentieth—the spirituality of the Catholic Church was molded to a very great extent by the spirituality of the "new" Orders: Franciscans, Dominicans, Carmelites, Jesuits. Each of these orders was founded or refounded by highly charismatic figures of profound sanctity: Francis and Clare, Dominic, Teresa of Avila and John of the Cross, Ignatius of Loyola. In every case, these founders or their associates produced an astoundingly rich mystical literature. It is breathtaking to think of what we owe to these traditions, especially in their first generations. The Franciscans gave us writers such as Bonaventure and Peter of Alcantara; the Dominicans, Thomas of Aquinas, Meister Eckhart, Tauler and Suso; the Carmelites, Teresa and John (and eventually Thérèse of Lisieux, Elizabeth of the Trinity, and Edith Stein); the Jesuits, Saint Ignatius in the sixteenth century and later, in the seventeenth and eighteenth centuries, a school of French mystical theologians such as Lallemant, Surin, and de Caussade.

All these orders, particularly in their masculine branches, were apostolic. They went on missions, staffed parishes, opened schools and universities, and exercised a widespread ministry of spiritual direction. They also extended their boundaries through the creation of third orders or "sodalities," by means of which lay people could be spiritually associated to a particular order and formed in its traditions. Putting all these factors together—the enduring influence of the founders (A *Time Magazine* report of October 15, 1992, declared Saint Francis one of the ten most important historical figures of the last thousand years), the schools of distinguished spiritual writers, the apostolic ministry of the priests and brothers (and eventually sisters), the receptivity to lay participation—it is no wonder that the thinking, sensibility, and prayer of most Catholics reflected the influence of one or another of these great orders. How many millions of Catholics spontaneously associated contemplative prayer with Carmelite prayer, looking to Teresa of Avila's *Interior Castle*, John of the Cross's *Dark Night of the Soul*, or Thérèse's *Story of a Soul* for inspiration and illumination?

How many other millions, both religious and laypeople, practiced for their whole adult life a form of prayer based on the *Spiritual Exercises* of Saint Ignatius? (It is worth recalling that numerous congregations, especially feminine ones, had Jesuits as their founders, and that these priest-founders naturally, almost inevitably, based the constitutions and spiritual practices of these new congregations on Jesuit models.) In short, during this entire period, the Catholic who wanted a life of prayer and devotion ended up drinking from the wells of one—or several—of these orders. This is all the more true in Brazil, where the work of colonization was accompanied right from the start by a work of evangelization, and this work was carried out almost exclusively by Franciscans and Jesuits. The fingerprints of the sons of Francis and Ignatius were everywhere, and their influence was all the greater because of the long-term prohibition placed by the Portuguese government on the establishment of men's contemplative communities—Cistercians, Trappists, Carthusians, Camaldolese— here in Brazil.

Over the last fifty years, however, a change has gradually been occurring. Laypeople, to whom the Second Vatican Council paid so much (and much-deserved) attention, without in any way turning their backs on their spiritual heritage, have begun to look in other directions for spiritual guidance and enrichment. One of the places where they have focused their attention is the monastic tradition. Since the decade of the sixties, an ever-increasing number of Catholics have been going on retreat to monastic communities. There they have encountered a way of spiritual practice and growth that seems to naturally correspond to their desires and their possibilities. They have "re-discovered" the psalms (the basis of monastic prayer from the third century) and made their own these poems of great beauty, immediacy, and intensity. They have dedicated themselves to *lectio divina*, the daily, prayerful immersion in the Word of God, in which a brief passage is meditated on for twenty or thirty minutes, allowed to connect with the inner heart of the reader, and then preserved for the rest of the day as a secret oasis to which the individual can always return, especially in moments of challenge, doubt, or stress. They have identified with the great honesty and realism of the monastic tradition, present especially in the *Sayings of the Desert Fathers* and the Rule of Saint Benedict, where monks talk with simplicity and humility about the difficulties of being a real Christian and of genuinely living according to the Gospel.

Many of these people have asked monks to be their spiritual directors and to initiate them into a tradition where silence and speech, communion and solitude, work and prayer, lightheartedness and seriousness, correction and pardon all have a place. Above all, they have been attracted to the monastic community— that assortment of ordinary, imperfect people, who commit themselves for their whole life to a single process, the process of learning to love: God, the neighbor, and themselves. They are entranced by the climate of peace, joy, and prayer that a community of un-special people succeeds in creating, simply by never giving up and by continually trusting in God's mercy. These laypeople understand intuitively why the first of the "Instruments of Good Works" in chapter four of the Rule of Saint Benedict is "To love the Lord God with your whole heart, your whole soul, and all your strength," and why the last is "Never lose hope in God's mercy."

This new interest in monastic spirituality has in its turn given rise to an ever-increasing body of monastic literature. Over the last half-century, many scholarly works have been written analyzing the doctrine of one or another classical monastic teacher. But the most notable growth has taken place in the emergence of a particular kind of monastic literature, which makes monastic wisdom accessible to the modern non-monastic reader, someone who wants to share in the riches of the monastery while continuing to be faithful to his or her vocation as husband, religious sister, seminarian, bishop, or single person. An impressive number of people in their forties, fifties, and sixties have found in monastic teaching the nourishment they were looking for. (I will never forget the woman who told me that before making contact with monastic spirituality she had been kept on a diet of tea and toast; now she experienced every day as a feast). Writers like Anselm Grün, Thomas Keating, Basil Pennington, John Main, Laurence Freeman, and Jean-Yves Leloup (to cite only a few) have found a large and appreciative audience. All of them are collaborators in this transmission of the Christian monastic tradition to the whole church. All of them have come to Brazil to present monastic spirituality personally and to help their readers and hearers appropriate it for themselves, as a way to intimacy with God, a way to universal charity, a way of transcending egoism, and ultimately, a way to joy.

I am grateful for this opportunity to offer my own response to the desire of so many people to know God more deeply through the path of monastic spirituality. In each of the brief chapters of this book, I will be presenting a particular aspect of the monastic search for God and experience of God. My hope is that it fits: that in the various practices, values, and insights described, you will recognize something that will bring you closer to your goal. Saint Benedict establishes as the only condition for receiving someone into the monastery a commitment to "truly seek God." The title of this book expresses my desire that my writing and your reading of these pages may be a way of seeking him—truly and together.

Bernard Bonowitz, OCSO
Mosteiro Nossa Senhora do Novo Mundo
Campo do Tenente

Part I

From the Rising of the Sun to Its Setting

Chapter One. Silence

In the introduction, I spoke about the interest that monastic spirituality has generated in the church in recent years. All kinds of people have discovered that instead of being an exotic lifestyle, radically different from that of ordinary Christians and intended for very few persons, the monastic way of being is very close to that of the common Christian, and its practices are easily incorporated into the daily life of all those who seek God. Naturally, they need to be adapted to the circumstances of the individual, but adaptation to particular needs is a monastic principle as old as the Desert Fathers of the fourth century.

The first practice that I would like to reflect on is silence. Perhaps my choice is due to the fact that monastic silence is one of the things that most draws the attention of those who visit a monastery or who come to make a retreat for several days. The retreatant is struck by the absence of sound, by the open spaces, by the strange phenomenon of a group of monks working together but not talking together. Another reason for my choice is the desire to undo the misconception that monks never talk—never—or that they bind themselves by a vow of silence. Monks do talk (sometimes more than they should!), and their commitment to limit their speech—Saint Benedict uses the word *taciturnity* (the inclination not to speak) in his Rule rather than *silence*—does not spring from an exterior commitment but from an intuition confirmed by experience. What is this intuition? We could describe it as follows: "Blessed are the silent, for they shall hear God."

This is what the monk wants when he refrains from speech. He wants to hear the voice of his Maker. At some point, he was a visitor or retreatant to a monastery, or a solitary hiker, or a patient in a lonely hospital room, and he made the discovery that for a brief moment, when his own voice ceased to dominate the atmosphere, instead of encountering a neutral emptiness, he heard Someone. Did he hear words, human words? Most probably not, although sometimes God makes his presence felt in the wrappings of human speech. He heard that Someone was there, and by the joy and the love and the awe that this hearing caused, he knew that this Someone was God.

Saint Teresa of Avila, in her description of the Fourth Mansions in the *Interior Castle*, likens this first experiencing of hearing God's wordless voice to that of someone hearing a distant shepherd playing a lovely melody on his pipes. It is the beginning of contemplation—the first gentle rumbling—and Teresa says that once a person has been privileged to capture a bit of this melody, to "drink of this water," as she says in a shift of metaphors, the only thing he wants is to go on hearing, to go on drinking. It may be that Teresa was inspired by Saint Augustine, whom she much admired, and who compared the experience of God in this life to the faint sound of ravishingly beautiful organ music passing through a door left slightly ajar: a little of the music of heaven that has made its way to earth, to the ears of a person of prayer.

It would not be wrong to say that frequently it is exactly this type of encounter that attracts people to the monastic vocation. They have heard God once, and their spontaneous reaction is "Encore!" They have discovered through various visits that the monastery is a place that favors silence and, to a certain degree, insists on it. They have come to the conclusion that the monastery is the context that will make possible a never-ending hearing of God. Who knows if one or another of them (a lover of English Romantic poetry, perhaps) is not thinking of the words of Keats: "Heard melodies are sweet, but those unheard / Are sweeter" ("Ode on a Grecian Urn")?

Unfortunately, there is a *however*; fortunately, this *however* is not absolute and can be overcome. It is the eventual discovery that the noise that makes hearing God difficult arises for the most part not from the sounds of the city, the sounds of one's associates, or even the sound of one's own human voice, but from the incessant sound of one's own inner orchestra. Paradoxically, as the young monk enters into the quieter rhythm of the monastic community, he becomes painfully aware of the fact that he himself is always talking, always talking to himself. About what? About his likes, his dislikes, his personal needs, and the human and spiritual limitations of the other members of his community. Poor young monk! He entered the monastery hoping for an unbroken dialogue between God and himself. His own voice would be the silent voice of his desire for God; God's voice would be the silent voice of the fulfillment of all his desires. Instead of this, the outwardly silent monk is faced with an uncontrollable monologue. Interiorly, he discovers, he goes on and on and on. No one can stop him—least of all himself. Now what?

The monastic tradition asserts that the cure resides in continuing to do what he is already doing. In other words, persevering in restraining outward speech to the truly necessary, he needs to endure the onslaught of his own noise without giving up on the desire of listening to God, the desire that led him into the monastic community. It is a constant monastic teaching that the person who guards a good measure of exterior silence and pays attention to what his inner voices are saying should be humble enough to share the demands of these inner voices with a spiritual director who can help him to interpret them. The content of this inner speech is not irrelevant, but it is meant to contribute eventually to his union with God. If the person keeps orienting and reorienting the attention of the heart to God, the voices will finally quiet down. The outward silence will then no longer stimulate an inward cacophony.

On the contrary, the outward silence will become a reflection of an inner silence, an inner tranquility. Exterior silence will no longer be a means to the attainment of inner harmony and the grace of hearing God's voice. It will be the echo of the inward silence, and inward silence in its turn will be the place where God is heard. This, according to the great monastic writers, is the wonderful time, when the human person walks habitually with God in the garden of Paradise, in total—wordless—communication. "Silence," says the great seventh-century monastic writer, Isaac of Nineveh, "is the mystery of the world to come" (*Ascetical Homilies*, 65). God willing, we will see many times in the course of this book that monastic life aims at being an anticipation of the world to come. Silence is one of these anticipations. In the quiet of the monastery, the quiet of the lips and the quieting of thoughts and desires, monks find the perpetual communion with God that they yearned for so intensely and for such a long time. What do they say now? What does their silence say? They repeat constantly in their heart the words of the young prophet Samuel in his first encounter with the living God: "Speak, Lord. Your servant is listening" (1 Sam 3:10).

I hope that this reflection has simply stimulated or strengthened a desire that already existed in the reader's heart. We know, as Christians, that we were made for communion with God—to see his face and to hear his voice. Many of you have passed through some experience of hearing the God who speaks without words, of the God who simply by being says "I am." This experience should not be thought of as a unique, once-in-a-lifetime occurrence; rather, it is meant to grow and expand until it includes the whole of our existence. The practice of exterior silence is a path to this ongoing communion. It does not have to be so intensely lived as within a monastery; probably it cannot be. But discerning choices can be made about the use of contemporary technology and face-to-face conversations. You can carve out small spaces of silence in your daily life, set aside for listening to God, for waiting for him to speak. Most probably this dedication will have its painful side, as it does in the life of the monk—the encounter with the inner dissonance, the conflict of discordant impulses and aspirations within ourselves. As ever, the way of wisdom consists in persevering in a spirit of faith. On the other side of noise, on the other side of the inner conflicts, are the unheard melodies that God plays on his shepherd's pipe—unheard but waiting to be heard.

Chapter Two. Prayer:
A General Introduction

What is it that monks do? These days, many Catholics ask the blessing of God through the intercession of Saint Benedict and have a medal with his image and a number of sacred texts. One of the best known of these is the motto of the Benedictines, which in a minimum of words resumes all of monastic activity in two verbs: *Ora et labora*. Pray and work. In the next few chapters, let us take a look at monks at prayer and discover as we do so that monastic prayer is in fact the heritage of all Christians.

Every monk by nature—and every human being as well—is both a cenobite and a hermit—a person who needs some form of community in order to truly be human, and a person who needs some measure of aloneness for the same reason—that is, to truly be human. God has constituted us in such a way that we can only attain and preserve our humanity if we respect both of these dimensions: communion and solitude. Too much community, and we begin to lose hold on our distinctive individual identity; too much solitude, and we begin to forget that we form part of a single human family, where every member is related to and responsible for all the others.

The monk reflects this inherent duality in his life of prayer. Every day, he dedicates himself for several hours to diverse forms of personal prayer—solitary meditation on the Word of God, silent prayer before the Blessed Sacrament, other forms of contemplative prayer in his cell. Even if he does his Scripture meditation in the monastery church or the common scriptorium, he is still engaged in personal prayer. He goes into his inner room, into his heart, and there he speaks to his Father in secret. On the other hand, every day the monk dedicates a number of hours to communal prayer. At the sound of the monastery bell, he leaves off whatever he may be doing—work or reading or private prayer or letter writing—and joins his brothers in the monastery church to give praise to God as a community in the Divine Office, the communal work of God. Private prayer is not more holy than communal prayer; communal prayer is not more powerful than private prayer. Together, they guarantee that the monk is slowly transformed into a person of prayer, a person who speaks to God face to face, sometimes in the company of his brothers or sisters, sometimes "alone with the Alone." If you asked a typical monk if he wouldn't prefer to give up common prayer in order to be able to consecrate the maximum of time to personal prayer—or vice versa—he probably would look at you as if you had some kind of spiritual or mental problem. He has learned through long years of practice that he is most united to God, to humanity, and to himself by this alternation—this alternation that has turned into his atmosphere, into the structure of his daily life.

Because of his constant engagement in these two modalities of prayer, the very manual labor that he performs during the remaining hours of the day also assumes the quality of prayer. The monk who is cleaning, cooking, painting, harvesting, working on the financial accounts, or preparing a class discovers with joy that this investment of time and energy is no less prayer than his moments with the Bible or his psalmody in the abbey church. It is no accident, I think, that the motto cited at the beginning of this chapter is put exactly in these terms: *Ora et labora*. The similarity of the words, their assonance, indicates that work is not something foreign to prayer, or prayer to work. *Labora* extends and incarnates *ora*: it is the prayer of the hands, the prayer of the body, just as *ora* is the monastic work par excellence, a working with the mind, the heart, the spirit, the voice in order to glorify God. All of this helps us to understand and appreciate that etymologically the word *monk* comes from the Greek word *monos*, "one." The monk is a man who strives to be one, the same, self-consistent person, in everything that he does and feels and thinks. This is his lifetime struggle, and it is also his glory, when this process of unification comes to fruition.

After this extended introduction, the first thing that ought to be said about monastic prayer, and indeed about all Christian prayer, is that it is born out of contact with the Word of God. Whatever form monastic prayer may assume, it is always inspired by the Word. In and through his Word, God communicates himself, his very life, to the human person, and prayer is nothing else but the free acceptance and appropriation of this divine life and its transforming consequences in the depths of the person to whom God speaks.

One way of considering the different types of monastic prayer is precisely by thinking about the ways in which the Word of God makes itself present. In the Divine Office—the common liturgical prayer of the community—the Word is present in an exuberant plenitude. What most dominates in the Divine Office is the verbal, the sung word and the spoken word. Every celebration of the Divine Office—traditionally called a liturgical hour—is composed of a cascade of words, almost all of them drawn from the Scriptures. The major part of each hour is dedicated to the chanting of a number of psalms, those sacred poems of the Old Testament that gather together all the sentiments of the human heart in its relation to God, oneself, life and death, nation and family, suffering, sin, and repentance. The psalms are often called "the prayer book of the Church," and whoever reads or sings them day after day learns truly and profoundly to pray. Little by little, such people make these texts their own and find in the psalms the spiritual vocabulary that enables them to communicate with God. In these poems, the man or woman of prayer finds words with which to present himself before God in every circumstance; in the psalms prayed in community, the monk concretely experiences how all Christians form a single body of Christ and how all of us basically have the same human heart, which needs to cry out to the Father in praise and pain and love and adoration.

In the case of the prayerful meditation on the Scriptures that we call *lectio divina*, the volume of text is much reduced. The monk in solitude chooses a brief passage of the Scriptures—often one of the readings of the Mass of the day—and slowly ponders it. Reading and rereading the same brief text for a half-hour or an hour, a world of meanings rises up before him—or better, rises up within him. The short text calls up other Scripture texts from within the monk's inner archive, or touches on personal experiences of his past or present, or leads him to a deeper insight into the person of Christ. Usually, one verse of the passage chosen remains with him throughout the day and constitutes a spiritual point of reference to which he constantly returns until the next moment of *lectio*.

When it comes to silent, personal prayer, often the number of words is reduced to a single phrase, perhaps even to a single word. Some words have content and resonance that are infinite—*God, Lord, love, glory, sin, peace, grace*. God can give such a word to a monk as a private treasure, and for years on end, in his times of personal prayer in the monastic daily round, the monk happily guards this word within his heart, either repeating it interiorly or simply saying it once and letting it be. He is led into an ever-greater identity with this word; in fact, his goal is to be made one with this word. But he happily acknowledges that however much time he spends with it, he will never exhaust its meaning.

Many Christians outside the monastery pray several hours of the Divine Office daily, or practice *lectio divina*, or engage in some form of simple, profound interior prayer. In their long-term participation in these practices, they have found the pearl of great price. The psalmist says, "To be near God is my happiness" (Ps 73:28). And what is prayer, if not "to be near God"?

Chapter Three. The Divine Office

Some years before entering the monastery I visited an exhibition of paintings by the French impressionist Claude Monet. Among the works of art displayed was a series of paintings of the cathedral of Rouen—twelve, if I remember. The first was "The Cathedral of Rouen at 7 a.m.," the second "The Cathedral of Rouen at 8 a.m.," and so forth. You might ask, "But what in the world was Monet doing?" He was celebrating the effect of light on matter, the transformation of matter that light produces simply by striking the same objects from different angles. He recognized, certainly, that in one sense what he painted and repainted always remained the same old cathedral. But he perceived that it was just as true to affirm that the movement of light created a new cathedral at least every hour. The impressionists were in love with light. And I think they were right to be so.

When we Christians celebrate the Divine Office—and *celebrate* is the proper technical term—we are doing something analogous to what Monet did with the church in Rouen. We are adoring the Divine Light—Christ, the Divine Wisdom—as it irradiates all creatures. In a way that surpasses natural light, the light of the Divine Wisdom calls things into being, nurtures them, leads them on to their full identity and then to rest. But rest is not the final moment. Sunset is not the end of the movement of the Divine Light. Because the light of God has shone on all creatures, they are destined to a second dawn, a resurrection. Monet, for all his genius, was unable to depict this. But Jesus Christ has painted the transfiguration of all creatures in the canvas we call Easter.

In the Divine Office, Christians worship the Divine Light—what the Orthodox call the "joy-giving light"—in three interlocking cycles: the day, the week, and the year. The first and the easiest to perceive is the cycle of the day. It is the cycle that has most in common with the work of Monet. The full Divine Office, as celebrated by monks and nuns in contemplative communities, begins long before the sunrise—in our monastery at three o'clock. Saint Benedict says of this first office, Vigils, "We arise at night to give God praise" (RB 16.5; see Ps 119:62). At this time we worship the invisible God, a transcendent God, and yet a God who is very near. We cannot see him at this hour, but we can feel him—we can reach out to him with our heart and feel him. Generally, the psalms and hymns of Vigils are sober and sometimes somber— they speak of a God who is the mysterious Lord of history, a just and holy God, and of the human person's attempt to correspond to this God by living uprightly and by remaining constantly in his presence. Here is a typical verse from a Vigils psalm: "The Lord is just and loves justice; the upright shall see his face" (Ps 11:7). The office of Vigils intersperses groups of psalms with two long readings, one drawn from the Scriptures and the other from the writings of the church fathers or another exponent of the church's tradition. In this sense, Vigils is our most substantial meal. What we hear in these two great readings, if we are really paying attention, is enough to keep our mind and spirit fueled for the rest of the day.

The Divine Light continues to move—Dionysius the Areopagite says that it is both always still and always in motion—and we encounter it again at the hour of Lauds. Lauds coincides with sunrise—with revelation, with the movement from the colorless to the multi-colored, to the rainbow. Creation exists before dawn, of course, but for us human beings that has to be taken on faith. At dawn, we see God's world. And this gift of the world renewed every morning draws forth from the Christian a response of praise and gratitude, even exultation. We know that Lauds means "Praises," and this is certainly the characteristic note of this moment of the Divine Office. The rhythm of the hymns passes from *lento* to *allegro*, and the psalmody of this office, whatever day of the week it may be, concludes with the final psalms of the Psalter, the so-called *Laudate* or "Hallelujah" psalms. Here is a sample: "Praise the Lord from the heavens, praise him in the heights. Praise him, all his angels, praise him, all his host" (Ps 148:1-2). Once the sacred psalmist gets going, he finds it almost impossible to stop. As we see, he begins by calling upon the angels and celestial powers to praise God. From there, he goes on to call the sun, moon, stars, fish, trees, and mountains to play their part in the worship of the Creator. Finally the psalmist tires of enumerating all the vast variety of creatures that he summons to praise God for his goodness and their existence. And so he ends with a sweeping general statement: "Let everything that lives and that breathes give praise to the Lord" (Ps 150:6). That is Lauds. And in this kind of spiritual climate, who can refrain from saying "Hallelujah"?

Morning and evening are the two great hinges of the diurnal cycle. One thinks of the initial chapters of Genesis: "And there was evening and there was morning—the first day." In fact, Lauds and Vespers (sung at sunset) are called the "cardinal" hours of the Divine Office, from the Latin word *cardo*, "hinge." But the Divine Office does not leap from morning to evening. Rather it moves serenely and tranquilly, and almost imperceptibly. The Christian follows the subtle trail of God's light, parallel to the path marked out for the sun. Between Lauds and Vespers, between morning and evening, there is the human day—the hours of productivity, the hours of collaboration and competition. This is the period of most intense physical and intellectual activity for the human being. For many people it is the real day, the opportunity we have to express ourselves and to make our mark in the world we live in.

The Little Hours of the Divine Office—Terce, Sext, and None—celebrated more or less at nine a.m., noon, and three in the afternoon—interrupt our activity a bit, but not to undermine it or to declare it unimportant. On the contrary, these briefer moments of the Divine Office (each lasting from ten to fifteen minutes) assure us that it is God's Spirit that gives us the will, the skill, and the energy to undertake our labor (Terce); it is God who at the moment of light's greatest intensity—noon—and work's greatest intensity as well calls us to a moment of spiritual repose and interior calm and invites us to renew our bodily forces with the food and drink we require (Sext), and it is God who returns to labor with us in the afternoon, but with a less hectic pace, as we and the world begin to slow down and to long for rest (None).

The psalms of the Little Hours are most frequently portions of the longest psalm of the entire Psalter, Psalm 119. This is a psalm that speaks in many different poetic ways of the Christian's desire to incarnate God's holy will in daily life. I imagine this as being one of the favorite psalms of Jesus, who desired in everything to "do the will of the One who sent him" (see John 5:30). And so it is a perfect psalm for this part of the day, when in addition to having the opportunity to make our mark, we are also given the possibility to act and interact in such a way that God's name is hallowed, his kingdom comes, and his will is done on earth as it is in heaven—through us, through our hearing his word and putting it into practice.

One might imagine that the monk or any Christian is just plain tired when he reaches the hour of Vespers. Interestingly, for most of the younger monks of our community, this is their favorite hour of the Divine Office. Even though as cloistered monks we work and live in the same place and don't need to commute, Vespers is a kind of homecoming. I think it is at this hour of the day (5 p.m.) that we return to ourselves, we enter into the house of our hearts, and we find God there waiting for us. The God of Vespers is a tender and loving God. It is true that he has been accompanying us with his light all through the course of the day, but now at Vespers he shows himself to us in a mild and loving light—the evening light—and draws us closer to himself. The Vespers psalms speak of God's faithfulness, of the care he has exercised on our behalf, of the victories that he has brought about in the lives of his servants in the day that is drawing to a close.

What marks Vespers most of all is the Song of Mary, the Magnificat, sung close to the end of Vespers every evening of the year. The Christian who sings the Magnificat identifies with Our Lady in her simplicity, her humility, her gladness. Mary sings, "All generations shall call me blessed, for the Almighty has done great things for me. Holy is his name." We know that we are not as holy as Mary, but all the same our heart overflows with peace and thankfulness at this time, and we believe that what is true for Mary is true for us as well: "All generations shall call me blessed."

There is one final moment, just before going to sleep—the office of Compline. It is a moment of self-entrustment, of confident abandonment, for those who "dwell in the shelter of the Most High, and abide in the shade of the Almighty" (Ps 91:1). Day has given way again to night; the series of Monet paintings has been completed. But we have been really and permanently changed by this day lived in the Lord's presence through our participation in the Divine Office. "May the God of peace himself sanctify you wholly" (1 Thess 5:23), we read at the Office of Compline. That is exactly what he is doing, day after day, every day, and we are able to recognize and give thanks for this in the celebration of the hours of the liturgy.

Chapter Four. *Lectio Divina*

We read in the Letter to the Hebrews, "The Word of God is living and active" (Heb 4:12). This brief affirmation contains the basic convictions with which we should place ourselves before and meditate on the Sacred Scriptures. In the first place, the Word of God is *living*. It is not a dead letter. Quite the contrary. It is a living Word addressed to us today. Our task is above all to allow the Word to speak to us, to permit it to make us ever more open and sensitive to its message, to learn the "art of hearing" that Martin Buber speaks about (in his *I and Thou*). Second, along with being living, the Word of God is *active*. Active in the fullest sense of the word: transformative. The Word of God is not satisfied with communicating information, insight, feelings, or even religious experiences to us—although it does communicate all of these. Its intention is to recreate us. Just as in the beginning God created the universe by his almighty Word, so now he intends to create us anew, create us for eternal life, through the power of his Word. Together with the sacraments, Scripture is the principal channel through which the grace of Jesus and the Holy Spirit comes to us and molds us.

I think this is what Jesus wishes to convey when he says that his words are "spirit and life." They infuse God's being and love and holiness into us and little by little turn us into new creatures. For the Scripture is *God's* Word; the Bible is *revelation*. Today it is clear to us that the Bible did not fall from heaven. Rather, it was composed over many centuries by many authors with clear influences from other cultures, and some of its passages were edited and reedited over the course of time. But this does not detract in any way from the reality of the Scriptures as revelation. Jesus, *the* Word of God, came to us in just the same way. Read the genealogies of Matthew's and Luke's gospels. Jesus himself did not fall from heaven. Many generations went into the making up of Mary and Joseph, Jesus' mother and foster-father, and thus, ultimately, into the making of the humanity of Jesus. Some of Jesus' ancestors were not of the chosen people, but were Gentiles.

That is how God works. He comes softly into our world, he blends himself with it. He makes himself human and the world divine. So the Scriptures are God's revelation in human vesture, in human language. That is what enables us to grasp them. But because they are God's Word, they should always be grasped with veneration and awe. My novice master in the monastery sometimes simply held the Bible to his heart during the time of Scripture reading, with an attitude of deep reverence and a beautifully tranquil smile. He had meditated on the Scriptures for many, many years, and now he was able to hear the text through his physical contact with it without having to open to a particular page. You and I are not there yet. But it is lovely to think that one day we might have such intimacy and familiarity with the Word of God.

Concretely speaking, *how* should we read the Scriptures? Is there a method that can be followed that will enable the Scriptures to penetrate us, convert and sanctify us? (The same passage from Hebrews with which we began this chapter goes on to say that the Word of God is "sharper than any two-edged sword"). I would say that there is no exact method. But there is a basic wisdom that the Church has—and perhaps the monastic tradition in particular—about the sacred interaction between the living Word and the human person. The name of this approach—*lectio divina*—has become fairly well-known in recent years. It is how monks describe their meditation of the Scriptures. It means "divine reading"—both in the sense that the content of what is read is divine and in the sense that the activity itself is divine: God speaking and I listening to him, God acting within my hearing so that I can grasp and assimilate and in a certain way become what I am reading. In general, the term is considered so rich and having so many overtones that most people prefer to leave it in Latin.

To begin with, *lectio divina* should begin with prayer, prayer to the Holy Spirit, God's light and God's wisdom. It is of the Holy

Spirit that the Creed says, "He has spoken through the prophets." We ask him, the primary author of the Scriptures, to give us a docile and understanding heart, to render us capable to hear exactly what he desires to say to us.

Having done this, we simply begin to read a short biblical passage. *Lectio* is not an occasional activity, but a daily one, and so it is good to have a continuity between today's passage and tomorrow's. Many people do their *lectio* on the gospel text of the Mass of the day. This approach can be especially rich if you attend Mass daily and will have the opportunity later on to hear proclaimed in the liturgy the same text that you reflected on before. Other people choose a book of the Bible and read it in its entirety over the course of several months. In either case, it is important that the text not be too long—never more than a chapter.

The reading is done slowly and with a brief pause between the verses (there is a wonderful fresco in Florence of Saint Dominic doing *lectio*, with his index finger on his lips as he pauses to interiorize the text, and a star over his head, symbolizing the illuminating grace of the Holy Spirit). It is not necessary to read to the end of the gospel passage or the chapter. As soon as you feel your attention and your heart touched by a phrase, a word, an image, that is a good place to stop. You are passing from the act of reading to what is called *ruminatio*.

Rumination or meditation is quietly abiding with the text that has stood out for you. This abiding usually takes place through a peaceful inner repetition of the word or words that have hooked you. One thing that I can guarantee is that those who read a Scripture passage slowly and unhurriedly will experience themselves being drawn to a given phrase—if not on the first reading, then certainly by the second or third. A particular word calls out to us: it wants to be lived with. It wants to be savored and chewed again and again by our inner palate (that's what *ruminatio* means, after all). Not by a process of hard thinking, not by trying to force a text to give up its treasures through applying all our intellectual abilities to it. No—but by the receptivity represented by repeating again and again, silently or audibly, the word that has touched us. It is in this way that the Word travels to our own personal depths, and from there it may call up other Scriptural texts from our memories to create new associations, or experiences from our past still in need of illumination (although we may not be aware of that need). Or the Word may be content just to find a home in us, and we may be content simply to hear the same word reverberate in us and challenge or console us—as in the case of Jesus' words, "Your sins are forgiven."

Frequently, a given time of *lectio* is taken up entirely with rumination. But it may happen that the divine Word provokes a profound response from us. We are focusing on one of the Beatitudes—"Blessed are the pure of heart," for example—and the desire that we have had for many years to possess this beatitude pierces us and pushes up from us a prayer that we did not compose, but that we ourselves *are* at that moment: "O God, make me pure of heart." Such a moment is called *oratio*. It is a prayer that the Holy Spirit has found in us, he the great deep-sea diver in our inmost depths, and in this moment of *lectio*, he prays it with us.

Something that does not happen every day in *lectio* (at least for me) but is always unforgettable when it does occur is the experience of *contemplatio*. Here the tradition is talking about a unitive contemplation—that is to say, when the Word being meditated on truly becomes event, reality, in the life of the reader. Imagine what it would be like if the promise of Jesus, "If anyone believes in me, he will keep my word, and my Father will love him and we shall come and dwell with him," actually became experience— if readers, not by effort, not by imagination, not by asking, but simply in the course of meditating on this word really came to experience within themselves the indwelling of the Father and the Son, the whole Trinitarian life going on *inside* them rather than outside them, and all this as a fruit and grace of contact with the living and active Word. *That* would be the fullness of *lectio*, where the act of reading becomes pure act, where Scripture *happens*.

Yet we should not think of these four moments—*lectio, meditatio* (or *ruminatio*), *oratio, contemplatio*—as a daily program to be worked through. God knows how he wishes to touch us with his Word and how he wishes us to respond to it. What counts is to love God's Word and more and more to let it fill not only the times of *lectio*, but all one's moments. As the Psalmist says, "Lord, how I love your law. It is ever in my mind" (Ps 119:97). Now *that* would make a good text for one's *lectio divina*!

Chapter Five. Personal Prayer: Listening to God

In our monastery, right after Vigils, the first hour of the Divine Office, we monks spend half an hour in church in personal prayer. What are we doing?

The Old Testament in the book of Numbers says that "God spoke to Moses face to face, as a man speaks to his friend" (Exod 33:11). In the first book of Samuel, the young boy Samuel says to the Lord, who has called him by name for the first time in his life, "Speak, Lord, for your servant is listening" (1 Sam 3:10). In the first book of Kings, God speaks to Elijah through a "tiny whispering sound" (1 Kgs 19:12). Personal prayer has something to do with all of these texts. It is being treated by God as a friend; it is attentive listening to the Lord who has invited us to a conversation; it is the perception of something very delicate and very subtle—something very close to silence—for that is how God speaks.

We can ask if this kind of prayer is for everybody, or only for a group of people (to whom we think we don't belong) who are called "mystics." To me, the clearest biblical response to this question is found in the early chapters of Genesis. There we read that every afternoon God took a walk in Eden, looking for his conversation partner, Adam, to talk with him and pass some time with him. "Adam, where are you?" "Adam," as we know, is not only a personal name of an individual; it also means, simply, "man," "human being." What God did with the first Adam, he desires to do with every son and daughter of Adam. "Adam, where are you? I'm looking for you." Prayer is letting ourselves be found by God, so he can speak to us—and, of course, so that we can speak to him, each one telling the other what is most personally important, and each one saying to the other through and behind the words, "I love you."

How can we learn to be found by God? I'm sure many of us are familiar with the book *The Little Prince* and with the great friendship between the prince and the fox. The fox is the prince's teacher of friendship; he explains to him that the best way to establish a profound relationship with a friend (which the fox calls "to tame") is to show up for an encounter every day at the same time. This is not only a sign of fidelity, says the fox. It also makes possible one of the great joys of meeting a friend—the joy of anticipation: "If for example you come at four o'clock, then at three o'clock I shall begin to be happy."

I'm sure that the fox was talking about four in the afternoon. As a matter of fact, we monks—a little strangely, perhaps—also arrive for our daily encounter with God at four o'clock—but at four in the morning, after the celebration of Vigils. In itself, the particular hour does not matter, but the fox is right in saying that a relationship of intimacy is constructed on the basis of daily fidelity. If we really wish to be found by God, we need to choose a certain time in our daily round and mark it out permanently for prayer: "This time belongs to God. From four to four-thirty [or whatever time you have picked out] I will wait for him here." I believe the fox is also right in speaking of the joy of anticipation. Anyone who has created a habit of prayer, a habit of being with God as friend with friend, looks forward with eagerness to that special moment. I think of a monk whom I knew many years ago who had difficulties with many aspects of the monastic life. "Why do I stay?" he once asked himself out loud as we were talking together. "I stay for the time of prayer in the morning. That makes everything else worth it."

Perhaps surprisingly, it is also helpful to have a regular place for the meeting with God. We know that "the Spirit of the Lord fills the world" (Wis 1:7), and yet all cultures have an intuition that there are sacred places—places that are holy because God manifested himself there, or places that become holy because they are set apart—consecrated—for intimate communion with God, whether through community prayer or personal prayer. When I came to Brazil in 1996 and entered the church of our monastery for the first time, the thought that immediately came to mind was "This place has really been prayed in." The daily prayers of the monks who had already lived here for almost twenty years before my arrival had created an atmosphere of prayer that clung to the wood, the stone, and the glass of the church. And the people who enter our church benefit from all the praying that has gone on. They know themselves to be in a house of God.

Back to our initial question: How can we learn to be found by God? How can we learn to listen to God? Basically the answer is, by practice and perseverance—and by desire. Whoever wants to be found by God *will* be found by God; whoever wants to hear his voice will develop a capacity to hear it, whether through the medium of words or without words. In the beginning, however, sitting still and trying to listen to God can be difficult. I believe that this difficulty is due in great part to the high level of anxiety that characterizes our present society. The whole interior side of the human person—reflection, thought, solitude, silence, the contemplation of beauty in art and poetry—has somehow become harder. We do not have the patience for it. Instinctively we look for conversation and noise and diversion. Yet waiting and patience are essential in learning to hear God speaking to us. As the prophet Isaiah says, "In waiting and in patience you shall be saved; in tranquility and rest lies your security" (Isa 30:15). And the twentieth-century mystic Simone Weil gave her most important book the title *Waiting on God*.

One practical way in which we can move towards an inner attitude of expectant waiting is by using what is frequently called a "prayer word." This is an ancient practice, dating already from the desert monks of the fourth century, and it also plays an important part in the beautiful fourteenth-century English treatise on prayer, *The Cloud of Unknowing*. We choose a single word or a short phrase—*God* or *Love* or *Jesus*—and we let it slowly reverberate in us during the time of prayer. By means of the gentle repetition of this word, the mind is quieted, the heart is focused, desire is intensified, the imagination calms down, and everything in us becomes ready to hear God as and when he wishes to speak. Most teachers of inner prayer recommend that the person praying leave pauses between each repetition of the chosen word, because this peaceful repetition, although beautiful and tranquil, is really still part of the preparation for prayer. The true praying will not consist in this repetition, but in the experience of hearing God in the heart. (By the way: this practice itself requires determination and patience. Maybe that is why one of the brief words that the author of the *Cloud* recommended was *Help!*).

It is typical—actually, inevitable—for those who seek to pray in this way to pass through the experience of distractions—to be visited by all kinds of irrelevant and worrying thoughts that have the potential of turning our attention away from God. All the great contemplatives insist that we should not let these distractions sadden us, or make us desist from praying. It is possible simply to observe them out of the corner of our eye—as if, standing on a bridge, we were watching boats going down the river beneath us (in a famous image drawn from oriental spirituality)—and simply let the river flow and the boats with it, while the center of our attention remains fixed on God. It is in this sense that we are to be like Mary rather than Martha: to be able to sit at the Master's feet and hear him without being overwhelmed by the preoccupations of our daily life.

The Russian Orthodox spiritual writer, Archbishop Anthony Bloom, once wrote that it is important to accept that God may sometimes leave us waiting and not show up. We will be there at the time of prayer; he will choose to be absent. For Bloom, this is one of the most beautiful and authenticating aspects of prayer. Prayer is a meeting of two free persons—God and ourselves. And just as we are not compelled to be present to God in prayer, so he is free to come and go as he chooses. This is the holiness and sovereignty of God, and all the more wonderful when he does choose to come and speak to our heart. What he says in such moments is unforgettable, is life, and light and medicine and nourishment (in the words of Saint Bernard), and the effects of what he says don't end with the end of the moment of prayer. They sustain and gladden us in the busyness and complexity of daily life. Slowly, they turn everything into peace.

Chapter Six. Work

Apart from eating and sleeping, the monastic day is taken up by the alternation of three principal activities: liturgical prayer (the Divine Office and Mass), personal prayer (including *lectio divina*), and work. In the last few chapters, we have reflected on public and private prayer. Now it is time to get to work!

Outside the monastery, work frequently receives a bad press. It is what we "have to do" in order to earn a living. It generates stress and frustration. It puts us under the control of bosses whom we have to obey, without necessarily respecting them. It is tiring. It doesn't correspond to our talents and aspirations. It eats up the major part of our time and leaves us only with the scraps—the few evening hours between arriving at home after work and the time when we need to go to sleep so that we can wake up with sufficient energy to go to work the next morning. What is good about work is that it generates money that makes possible other, very different, activities: leisure, vacations, trips, restaurants. Work, in short, is often considered as the heavy price we pay for the times when we don't work.

It is true, of course, that work has a certain penitential aspect. When we read Genesis 3, we find it was as a punishment for sin that Adam was told that hereafter he would have to "eat his bread in the sweat of his brow." But I am certain that God is not such a hard taskmaster as it might seem, and that work was always in his loving plan for us, long before sin entered the world. God himself, according to Jesus in the Gospel of John, is "always at work" (John 5:17), and Jesus takes the Father as a model for his own work of salvation on our behalf. We need to re-discover work as a gift rather than as a necessary evil. So we ask, "What's good about work?"

In the monastery, one of the first things a young monk learns about work is that it is an opportunity to form our character and our personality. This is one of the great graces and responsibilities of being human: that we are allowed to give a shape, a form, to who we are precisely by what we do. In this sense, all work is primarily work on ourselves. There are many virtues (and virtue is the moral beauty of the human person) that are acquired primarily through work: carefulness, the quest for excellence, perseverance, attention, the ability to transcend our moods in order to fulfill a task, the cultivation of calmness and steadiness as the appropriate emotional environment for work, the development of capacities that would otherwise remain latent.

Here in the monastery, for example, we do our own cooking. Fine. But almost every young man who enters has no idea of how to cook. What happens? He *learns*. He is placed for a few months, once or twice a week, as assistant cook, in charge of the salad. But at the same time, he is introduced to the mysteries of rice and beans by the principal cook. And six months later, more or less, he graduates to becoming one of the head cooks himself, capable of forming new apprentices. This example brings to mind the fact that work is also a school of social, interpersonal virtues. In our community, work is the area that generates the greatest number of arguments. Personally, I consider this totally natural. Collaboration, give and take, the ability to give orders and to obey—these qualities are not innate; they are learned through work in common. Moreover, they are indispensable, especially when the people you work with are not strangers or mere colleagues, but the brothers of your religious family, and the boss is not an anonymous master but rather your spiritual father.

Closely related to this dimension of work is the idea that it is a vehicle for self-expression, a chance to "enact ourselves," to "express ourselves." We may find this notion easy to accept in reference to so-called creative work: the work of a composer, an inventor, a writer, a statesman, a psychologist. As a matter of fact, however, almost all work is creative. There *are* limited situations— in prisons, concentration camps, etc.—when people are given brutal and senseless work to do, as a way to humiliate them. But this very possibility only highlights the truth that apart from such cases, work of its nature involves creativity. There are many ways to sweep a church, to wash the dishes, to cut the grass, to paint the walls of the gift shop—and in the midst of all these ways is your particular way, the way that is natural and efficient and playful for you, the way that removes the opposition between work and pleasure. It is one of the joys of monastic work (and I see no reason that it cannot be so outside the monastery) to find your own way: to discover your own rhythm, your own method, your own approach to realizing a given task. Once people get the knack (not a universal knack, but their own knack), work is no longer deadening but enlivening. Take my word for it—the word of someone who spent five years working in a monastic jelly factory!

The ancient monks who invented the idea of the monastic tripod (liturgical prayer, personal prayer, work) understood that as dynamic beings we need physical activity, and that this physical activity can be a fruitful environment for our ongoing spiritual life. No one is capable of praying psalms sixteen hours a day or remaining in the chapel for long stretches of time without a break. It doesn't correspond to our psychological makeup. The interlude of work, performed in a peaceful, regular manner, does not interrupt our union with God. On the contrary, it provides another ambience for the continuation of our attention to God. Most tasks are not totally absorbing: even when we give them the concentration they deserve, they still leave a certain part of our mind free.

What shall we do with this freedom? Many people "tune in" to their own emotions and have long inner monologues, frequently repetitive and not very productive; others listen to music for hours at a time; others engage in constant conversations with their co-workers. But there also exists the possibility of allowing this space of freedom in the midst of our tasks to function as room for reflection. Paradoxically, in requiring part of our attention, work allows what remains to focus fruitfully on God, on one's own life, on a Scripture passage, on the needs of other people. The physical work somehow liberates our thinking. Often enough, our most profound intuitions come to us in the middle of performing a simple, apparently unrelated, task. The Buddhists understand this fact, and so work is an important component in their spiritual program. But I believe that the housewife knows this as well, and the carpenter, the electrician, and the gardener. The only condition for experiencing this spiritual contact in the midst of work is some degree of silence.

At its highest, work can enable us to compose our own "Canticle of Creatures." We are all familiar with the ecstatic poem composed by Saint Francis toward the end of his life, when he praised the Lord for sun and moon, fire and water, life and death. When we work, we have a more intimate, immediate, hands-on contact with the marvels of creation. Work enables us to appreciate wood, iron, cloth, stone. As we fashion them, they reveal their beauty and their dignity to us. One of the sources of income in our monastery is the production of honey. Sometimes I envy the monks who work in that department. It is they who experience daily the docility of honey, its sweetness, its nourishing effects, its medicinal qualities. Or the monks in our bakery, who live with their hands in the dough. We touch the creation directly in our work. And whenever the creation is touched, it speaks of God.

Finally, work furnishes us with the joy of being generous. The birthday present you buy, the flowers you send your mother or your grandfather, the concert tickets you give to a friend are precious because they are the fruit of your labor. As human beings we need to have visible ways of showing love—flowers, presents, tickets—and the payment we receive for our work can be (should be) invested in symbols of affection. In our own case, our monastic constitutions tell us that a part of the receipts of the monastery should be set aside for the poor. Right from the beginning of Christian monasticism it was understood that the monk was to work for his own sustenance and in benefit of the poor. That is truly one of the great blessings of work: it enables us to be our brother's keeper. Cain thought that being his brother's keeper was a heavy and unjust task imposed on him by the Lord. He was wrong. It is a privilege.

Chapter Seven. Asceticism

According to many monastic writers, the fundamental ascetical challenge is the *unification of desire*. Desire is the dynamic element of our journey to God; it is the energy that gets us off and running towards God, rather than merely sitting still, in the vague hope that one day God will drop by and visit us. Saint Augustine wrote in his *Confessions*, "My desire is my weight" (13.9.10)—that is, the gravitational force that impels me towards the object that I yearn to possess. And Meister Eckhart, expressing the same intuition but in his own original way, affirmed in his *Talks of Instruction*, "The greater the thrust of my will, the greater my love."

So, as far as it depends on us to get to God, desire is the fuel that enables us to journey. The early church fathers and monastic writers teach that initially the desire of the human person was completely unified. Each human being desired one thing and one thing only—God. God attracted and magnetized all our desire. All that we wanted was to love him, serve him, see him, and be happy with him forever.

Original sin changed all this by fragmenting our desire. In a powerful image, Saint Bernard speaks of sin as the hammer that shattered our desire into a million pieces. It did not destroy it— desire is ineradicable in the human soul—but it did disperse it to the four winds. And the result is that we do not desire *anything* with our whole heart, our whole soul, our whole mind, and our whole strength. Yes, we can experience strong gusts of desire— even hurricanes of desire—for a given object. But these storms usually blow themselves out very quickly, and we lose interest in that which for a brief moment we desired so intensely. Soon enough, our desire is attracted to another object that promises us satisfaction.

With such a divided faculty of desire within us, the ancient Christian monks asserted, we will never make it to God. Any obstacle will be enough to discourage us; any delay in the fulfillment of our yearning will suffice to dissuade us. The journey to God can only be accomplished when we are functioning with the full stock of our desire. Somehow or other, we will need to discover a method that succeeds in summoning back into unity all the shards of our desire. What method?

The monks hit upon a manner of proceeding that can appear paradoxical, because at first glance it seems to aim at the diminution of desire rather than its intensification. The method is called *detachment*, and the term is perfect for the reality it describes. Detachment is a program of removing the tentacles of our desire from the myriad of objects that they reach out to. Bit by bit, one by one, we succeed in undoing the attachment we experience for a multitude of things, persons, pleasures, and experiences. But what is the point? The point is that every time we detach a fragment of our desire from a particular object, that fragment becomes liberated, accessible, capable of being united to our underlying desire for God, and thereby capable of intensifying and strengthening this fundamental desire for the Divine. The monks of antiquity believed—and contemporary monks still do believe—that if it were possible to detach our desire from everything that is not God, then automatically all our desire would be able to be dedicated to the search for God. *Then* we would truly have a stock of desire sufficient to get us to our journey's end, and we would "run to God, with hearts expanded, in the ineffable sweetness of love" (Rule of Saint Benedict, Prol. 49).

That's the theory. The practice is a little more difficult. However divided our desire may have become, desire remains desire, and once it twines itself around an object, it does not easily let go. Desire has accustomed itself to find many sources of satisfaction, and it is unwilling to be deprived of any one of them. This means that the reunification of desire will necessarily have to be a battle, with our profound, underlying desire for God fighting to reclaim the territory it has lost to a host of other desires—desire for physical pleasure, desire for possessions, desire for power, desire for the admiration of others, desire to be the center of the universe, desire for security.

Asceticism is this concrete battle for the reunification of desire. It is the daily implementation of the theory of detachment. Asceticism recognizes that at the beginning—and perhaps for a good while—our multifaceted desires will continue as strong as ever, becoming even stronger when we do not comply with them. Asceticism does not insist on an immediate liberation from the multiplicity of our desires. It simply says to them, "You're not going to get what you ask for, even if you kick and scream. The energy that you are absorbing belongs to the great endeavor of seeking God. Your owner can't get to God unless you eventually let go. So like it or not, let go!"

Usually, the desires don't like it. One saying of the Desert Fathers compares them to snakes that, when satisfied with the milk they crave—the objects they are attached to—go to sleep in the sun and don't show their fangs. Deprived of their habitual satisfactions, the desires become enraged and make their impulses felt in a constant and almost terrifying way.

With this, you, the reader, now understand why we monks fast, why we get up so early in the morning, why we speak only insofar as is necessary, why we do not buy what we want but only what we need, why we don't have television or radio, why we don't go on vacation, etc. We are engaged in the battle of reclaiming our dispersed desire so that it can all be applied to the continual search for the face of God. Do we sometimes feel an inner resistance to all of this self-negation? Do we ever! Do we sometimes question whether it will ever be possible to put together all the broken bits of glass? Absolutely! But we do know, without doubt, that we go to God on the wings of desire, and that we need all the desire we can muster—all our own desire. For that reason, many times we say "no" to ourselves, always within the context of the great "yes" that we say to God.

Anyone who practices asceticism in any genuine degree (I forgot to mention that the word is etymologically related to *athlete*) will need to have a good spiritual director. Strangely enough, asceticism itself can become a new and intensely powerful attachment. Every monk is familiar, whether through personal experience, observation of his fellow monks, or reading, with cases where an ascetic fell in love with his own asceticism. Gradually, fasting became more important than the search for God, or absolute poverty, or an unbreakable silence, or the sacrifice of as many hours of sleep as is humanly possible. God got lost in the process, and the ascetical project turned into the new object of desire.

This result is due to another quirk of our fallen human nature—our almost insuperable orientation to ourselves. Extreme fasting, simplicity, silence, and vigils are all variant forms of self-adoration, all forms of pride—and any one of them can become compulsive. That is why a good spiritual director is indispensable, someone who can tell the monk honestly and firmly that he is really exaggerating and that he has gotten off the high road that leads to God only to end up in some unproductive detour. The monks recommend two basic rules for discerning the just measure of asceticism: 1) Aim at the midpoint between excess and defect, whatever the focus of your asceticism may be. 2) Take *necessity* as your guideline in eating, drinking, sleeping, talking, and everything else. If you abandon the solid principle of the necessary, you will end up giving in either to the endless craving for superfluity or to the infinite craving for self-abnegation. Put in the simplest terms, we could say that the true ascetical path leads neither to obesity nor to anorexia.

Monks continue to practice asceticism in the twenty-first century because they personally know people who by grace and human effort have succeeded in having one desire and one only (I love the title of Sören Kierkegaard's book on the sacrament of confession, *Purity of Heart is to Will One Thing*). Having one desire, these people are brought to the attainment of what they are seeking—the treasure in the field, the pearl of great price, the kingdom of God, God himself. If you've ever known a person like that, and you have a monastic heart, then all that you want is to become like that person: to desire God and to possess God—and of course to be possessed by him. And at the journey's end, there is an unexpected blessing (already promised by Jesus in the Gospel): Whoever leaves all things for God's sake ends up not only finding God but having restored to him everything that he renounced. Once God is our only desire and our prize, he gives back to us everything that we gave up for him, because he knows that from now on nothing can ever separate us from his love.

Chapter Eight. *Otium Sanctum*

Over the centuries, the monastic authors created a vocabulary of religious and mystical experience. One of the most beautiful entries in this dictionary of monastic spirituality is *otium*: in English, "leisure, holy leisure."

Latin distinguishes between *otium* and *otiositas*, between inner (and outer) repose and just plain laziness. The latter, according to Saint Benedict, is "the enemy of the soul"; the former, we could say, is its best friend.

Otium is, in the first place, a state of soul—a peacefulness, a freedom from preoccupation, a quiet receptivity to life, and a resting in what life brings. It is the Sabbath aspect of human and monastic life. It is what we do or how we are when our work is done. When we have completed a given task, the pause that follows is not simply the time necessary to regroup our forces for the next task. The pause is not a time of emptiness but of fullness, time for savoring what life is, independent of our responsibilities and accomplishments.

I used the word *time* twice in the last sentence, and, in fact, true *otium* is not possible without time set apart for it. A lasting state of inner rest requires long moments free from obligations—financial, intellectual, interpersonal. When we read the gospels and the disputes between Jesus and the Pharisees, we can be led to think that the Old Testament went overboard in its prohibitions of so many different activities on the Sabbath. In fact, however, the intention of the laws concerning the Sabbath was precisely to guarantee the possibility of a genuine *otium* for the people of God. Of course there are emergencies that require breaking the Sabbath—such as the healings that Jesus realized—but apart from these exceptions, it is wonderful that biblical spirituality took pains to preserve a time of inner and outer rest for the human person. "Remember the Sabbath Day, to keep it holy" (Exod 20:11). God considered this precept so important that he included it in the Ten Commandments.

What are some typical experiences of monastic *otium*? Certainly the moments of personal prayer and reading scheduled in the course of the monastic day are opportunities for refreshment. They are moments apart with God, of blessed solitude, as the medieval tradition expressed it. But fortunately, the monastery provides other occasions for *otium*. The good monk knows how to enjoy them.

One of the most universal ways for the monk to be re-created through the experience of *otium* is in the encounter with nature. On a Sunday afternoon or on a workless solemnity, whatever the season, whatever the weather, you can always find a monk taking a long, solitary stroll on one of the roads of the monastic property. (I am frequently one of them). Perhaps it is the road that runs between the two small lakes near the entrance to our monastery; perhaps it is the long tree-shaded path that leads to the area set apart for reforestation; perhaps it is an excursion into the dense underbrush, where it is not impossible to get lost. (As a matter of fact, I myself have lost my way on several occasions and have needed to be rescued by a monastic search party.)

Whatever the road, the monk's heart expands as he ambles along it. He is naturally and quietly attentive to everything—the color of the butterfly's wings, the height of the growing wheat stalks, the complex song of a forest bird that sounds for all the world like a Scottish highland melody right here in southern Brazil. The monk is in communion with all this, by looking and by listening. Once in a while he will find an especially interesting stone and put it in his pocket to bring back to the monastery; once in a while he will pick a wild flower or a leaf and carry it with him for a while, only to drop it at a later moment. But basically, he is not souvenir shopping. He is in the world's greatest museum—the natural world—and he feels no necessity to buy anything in the gift shop. Over the years I have come to believe that this is a universal hallmark of the monk—a spontaneous joy in nature, a deep, silent appreciation of what God has made, and a silent gratitude to the One who has made it. If it is possible to envy oneself, I believe that we monks envy ourselves for the natural beauty that surrounds us and to which we open our eyes especially wide at the times of *otium*.

Otium does not necessarily mean that the monk doesn't use his hands or his brains. Personally, I have a remarkably small quantity of manual talent, but our community abounds in people who are good with their hands. So if, like me, you head down to the lake, rosary in hand, and you pass by the different workshops leading away from the main buildings to the principal road, you will almost surely hear someone banging away with a hammer or see someone whittling a small statue or hear someone practicing scales on a flute. I don't know if there exists in Portuguese the simile *happy as a lark*, but that is a good description of the happiness of these monks. They are peacefully immersed in some simple activity that fulfills them and puts them in touch with the springs of their inner life. Paradoxically, they are at the same time completely unselfconscious and profoundly happy. They are not thinking about themselves, but about the wood, the stone, the metal with which they are working or the music they are playing. They are solemnly and playfully absorbed in what they are doing, without distraction, without worry, without care for what the next day will bring. They are all attention.

Many years ago, an older monk at my first monastery, one who worked with the farm animals, took me to the sheepfold and told me to look at them for a good long time. After having my look, I asked him why he had brought me. "Bernard," he answered, "you have to learn to think like a sheep, to simply let go of yesterday and tomorrow and live now." As I say, that was many years ago, and although I was impressed by the older monk's words, I can't say that I understood them then. Even today, it seems to me that my appreciation for his wisdom remains incomplete. But I am happy to say that as the years go by I am becoming more sheep-like.

Up to now, I have described *otium* as if it were always something to be lived in solitude. That is, without doubt, an authentic aspect of *otium*, but *otium* also has its social dimension. And the social dimension of *otium* is friendship. Two or more monks can set out on an afternoon hike to experience the same beauty of nature together that another has chosen to experience alone. As they pass by the lakes, the wheat, the birds, they may wish to add their own voices to this gentle chorus, telling each other something about their spiritual life, or their struggles or their joys. Probably, after a short burst of conversation, they will lapse into silence, preferring to let nature do the talking and themselves do the listening. At such a moment, the friend is another blessed presence, another testimony to the reality of God that permeates all existence.

The Carthusians do this once a week. The whole community sets out on a *spatiamentum*, a walk like that of Jesus and his disciples, where the nearness and the beauty of the kingdom of God makes itself felt. A wonderful Italian Renaissance painting, *Paradisus Claustralis* ("Monastic Paradise"), beautifully captures this communion in *otium*. In it, clusters of monks in a Tuscan countryside are depicted sitting or standing, conversing or silent, gazing inward or gazing at each other, and all bathed in that Italian Renaissance gold that symbolizes holiness and happiness and peace. This tradition goes all the way back to the first Christian monk, Saint Anthony the Great, who once in a while took his disciples out for a long purposeless hike—to "make the bowstring of the monastic life less tense," as he put it; to relax, as we would put it (*The Sayings of the Desert Fathers, Alphabetical Collection*, "Anthony," 13).

I hope that reading these pages has left you with your mouth watering. You must know the famous sentence in Augustine's *Confessions* where he speaks of the restless human heart, created to rest in God. *Otium*, in its many different forms, is a foretaste of that rest. In fact, it is God in the flower, in the flute, in the friend that makes *otium* an experience of newness of life, a little resurrection. It is God touched and held and briefly possessed in the diverse forms of *otium* that makes this repose into something genuinely holy. In the pause and peace of *otium*, I find and feel the God whom I am always looking for.

Chapter Nine. Community

It is possible for a monk to think of community in a purely instrumental way: the community is the supportive context that I need in order to lead the kind of life that brings me to God. In this case, the community supplies the indispensable *structures* for my journey to God. It furnishes me with an ordered, balanced round of activities—liturgical prayer, manual work, private prayer—that I practice faithfully, motivated by the faithful practice of the brothers who surround me. It guarantees an atmosphere of recollection, silence, and solitude favorable to seeking the face of God. It frees me from having to dedicate much of my time and energy to financial and administrative concerns. I work for a given number of hours a day, but I don't have to worry about bills, checking accounts, budgets: there is a small team of monks in the community that assumes that responsibility and thus liberates me from it. Through the abbot's daily teaching, the community offers me spiritual inspiration and a call to grow in depth; through his corrections (and those of other senior brothers), the community watches over my spiritual growth and keeps me from going off the deep end. The community has a library of good spiritual books to develop my intellect and my devotion. The community offers me sufficient affective nourishment through the fraternal life that I can persevere in what is an essentially solitary path.

Or it is possible to think of the community in a more teleological way. In this case, the community goes beyond being simply a means and, together with God, becomes a central goal of the monastic life. My novice master used to say that the monk is committed to two "ecstasies." He has to strive after the vertical ecstasy of going out of himself and into God, and he also has to strive after the horizontal ecstasy of going beyond individualism into genuine *koinonia*—"sharing of life"—one of the most common classical descriptions of a monastic community. According to my novice master, true self-transcendence requires this double exodus out of self-centeredness. You can't choose one or the other; it has to be both.

There is a wonderful book by the Jesuit theologian and cardinal Henri de Lubac that supplies the intellectual basic for this twofold movement out of self and into union with the Other and with others. The book is called *Catholicism: The Social Aspects of the Dogma*. In it, de Lubac explains that just as original sin involved two ruptures of communion, so salvation involves two reconstructions of communion. In original sin, he says (drawing on many texts from the fathers of the church), the human person not only distanced himself from God (Adam hiding in the garden from the God with whom he had previously conversed on a daily basis); he also distanced himself from his brothers and sisters. Disobedience to God on the part of Adam and Eve completes itself, as it were, in Cain's murder of his brother Abel. Human beings become God's enemies by the rejection of his loving fatherhood; they become enemies of one another through the denial of their brotherhood.

This is not the world God wants, de Lubac asserts. What God desires is the restoration of both unities, both communions: between God and humanity and between man and man. And the realization of this double reconciliation is the reason that the Father sends Christ into the world. It is Christ's immense and indispensable task to reconcile humanity with God, and, equally important, to reconcile human beings among themselves. Christ accomplishes our reconciliation with God through his paschal mystery—his suffering, death, resurrection, and sending of the Holy Spirit. He accomplishes our mutual reconciliation with one another through the establishment of the church. Yes, the church is the society of those reconciled with God who are called to grow into an ever-more profound and complete unity with each other. "That they may be one": so Jesus prayed at the end of the Last Supper (John 17:11). This is what de Lubac means by talking of the social aspect of the dogma. Catholicism is not a one-person-at-a-time project, whereby each person is saved in and for himself.

Catholicism is a social project whereby the Church dedicates itself to achieving simultaneously the unity of humanity with God and the unity of the whole human race. Cyril of Jerusalem says that "God created the universe with the church in mind" (*Mystagogical Catecheses*). This is not triumphalism. It is Cyril's way of saying that the end purpose of creation is a humanity reconciled in itself and reconciled with its creator: a civilization of love of God and of love of neighbor.

This brings us back to the monastery. If one of the traditional names for a monastery is *koinonia*, another is *ecclesiola*. A monastery is, literally, a little church, a mini-church, a local expression of the universal church, endowed in a particular way with the diverse gifts and charisms of the great church. As such, the monastery has the same two interrelated obligations to its members: to help each monk grow in ever-greater communion with God and to help each monk grow into ever-greater communion with the brethren. It is only in this way that a monastery really sanctifies its members.

Now this can be a good deal harder than it looks. Although monks are by and large decent human beings, persons with high ideals and generosity in carrying them out, persons who recognize Christ as their savior and God as their center, they are in general pretty individualistic, often more so than the average person outside the monastery. It is not solely for spiritual motives that a monk chooses a life without wife and children, a life lived far from the city and the means of communication, a life of little speaking and much silence and solitude. Inevitably, along with the spiritual motives, there is a psychological predisposition that makes a person feel attracted to a monastic vocation. The psychological factor does not invalidate the reality of the spiritual quest. It can, however, render difficult what my novice master called the "horizontal ecstasy"—leaving self and the preferences of self behind for the neighbor—for all the neighbors—that is to say, for the community.

So the common life has something of asceticism about it, as every path of self-transcendence does. Not a day goes by in the monastery where each monk is not called to forget himself for the sake of the common good. As an individual, the monk (like all

human beings) has his own way, his own attractions and repulsions. As a human being, he inevitably experiences these same
attractions and repulsions with regard to the other members of
his community. Some he finds automatically *simpático*; others he
comes to find *simpático* only in the course of time, with the help
of a lot of prayer and good will; others he will never experience
as *simpático*. Yet as a monk, he knows that he is called to love and
serve all of them, the *simpáticos* and the *antipáticos*, and to con-
struct with them a genuine Christian community. This enterprise
can be so demanding that there are canonized saints who have
bluntly declared that the greatest penance of community life is
community life itself. When the French Orthodox theologian,
Olivier Clément, reserved the final chapter of his great book *The
Roots of Christian Mysticism* to the treatment of the love of the
brethren, describing it as "the difficult love," he was saying much
the same thing.

Is there a secret to succeeding in this venture? There are two.
The first is a gradual discovery of one's personal identity within
the communion of the community. In the long run, the purpose of
all this self-transcendence is not (absolutely not!) self-destruction
for the sake of some common good. Rather, it is a profound and
joyful experience of oneself as a person in communion. Slowly
and arduously, the monk learns the reality of the we. He is not
destined—condemned, one might say—to be an I in isolation; he
is invited and formed to be a living member of a community of
persons—the Body of Christ of his local monastic church.

And this is where the second secret comes in. The labor involved in moving from isolation to communion is not essentially
moral, but mystical. What is at stake is not the conquering of
selfish habits in order to become a good monastic citizen; instead,
the monk is participating in the "trinitarianization" of humanity.
It is Augustine who teaches us that man is the image of God not
so much as an individual, but as a society, a society of persons
willingly permeable to one another (*Exposition on the Psalms*,
Psalm 132). When a monastic community lives a constant cycle
of love and service and generosity, that community makes the
Holy Trinity present and visible here on earth. That community
is a foretaste of the kingdom of God.

Chapter Ten. The Abbot—
and Other Fathers

It is not without reason that having treated the theme of community we pass on to considering the spiritual function of the abbot. Years and years of monastic life make one think spontaneously along the lines of the Rule of Saint Benedict. In it, Benedict dedicates the first chapter to the kind of community he envisions. The second forms a kind of job description of the abbot's role in this monastic community.

Saint Benedict says the most important thing about the abbot right at the beginning of the chapter: "The abbot is believed to hold the place of Christ in the monastery" (RB 2.2). In the early Church, Christ was venerated as father of his people as well as their brother, and so was often referred to as *abba*—the Aramaic for *father*. This particular title of Christ—the title that affirms his spiritual fatherhood—came to describe the superior of a monastic community. *Abbot* is simply the English form of *abba*.

How does the abbot fulfill his task of fathering the brethren? To father is to beget, direct, and empower life, and it is precisely this that constitutes the abbot's responsibility. He has to generate and cultivate spiritual life in each and all of his sons. Naturally, he himself is not the author of this life. He is, Benedict says, "believed to hold the place of Christ in the monastery"—to exercise the mission of Christ in the monastery—but he is certainly not believed to be Christ, one hopes not even by himself!

No, he is a living channel of Christ's life, doing his best to maintain himself open to the wisdom, grace, and inspiration of Christ's Holy Spirit, and seeking to impart this wisdom and make it effective in the members of the monastery, in all the aspects of their communal life. We could say that that reaches from the most practical and concrete to the most spiritual and sublime, but it is part of Benedict's genius to see that these two categories are not separate but in continual, fruitful interaction.

According to the Rule, the abbot's first way of carrying out his mission is through *teaching*. He is the principal teacher in the monastic community, and his textbook is the Bible. Every day he is to instruct the brothers in the knowledge of the Scriptures, opening a new approach, casting a new light, inviting toward a more profound perception. Like a good baker, he is to "knead this knowledge of the Scriptures into the minds of his disciples" and let the sacred texts "leaven" their intellect and their outlook.

The abbot should extend this work of teaching throughout the day by the example he gives, by his fidelity to the monastic way of life. Learned monks, says Saint Benedict, may perhaps be able to profit from sound intellectual instruction even when the abbot does not reinforce his teaching by personal example. The great majority of the monks, however, will be looking to see what the abbot does and will end up putting that into practice—for better or for worse. This is one of the curious and distinctive features of a Benedictine monastic community. Benedict has made the role of the abbot so central that the abbot can't help profoundly influencing the brothers by his way of embracing the joys and obligations of monastic living. Like father, like sons. In a monastic community, there's no way of getting around this.

The strong interior dimension of monastic life makes it imperative for the abbot to be conscious of, and responsive to, individual needs. In speaking of the abbot as a spiritual *guide*, Benedict recognizes the necessity of a personalized approach. This, in fact, will be one of the most challenging parts of the abbatial ministry: the need to adapt himself to a variety of personalities and spiritual attitudes. The abbot will have to be very attentive in order to be able to authentically grasp the type of person he is dealing with. According to Saint Benedict, some monks for the most part require only occasional encouragement to continue on the good path on which they are traveling. Others need a stronger stimulus, because of having lost, at least temporarily, the "good zeal" that should inform their monastic practice (see RB 2.25; 72.2). (This loss is not surprising: monastic life is a long haul, and almost everyone passes through periods of lack of enthusiasm and the temptation to minimalism that accompanies it.) Still others may be engaged in truly anti-monastic or even anti-Christian attitudes and behaviors. For these monks, the abbot has to lay down the law. They are putting themselves and other brothers whom they might lead astray at risk. Whatever the type of monk, Saint Benedict is clear that each of the brethren merits loving and respectful treatment. Even when the abbot has to be stern, this strictness must respect the brother's dignity and should never express itself in contempt, irritability, irony, or coldness. Here we return to the foundational principle: "The abbot is believed to hold the place of Christ in the monastery." If this holding of Christ's place is to be truly credible, then the abbot has to make his daily behavior a true imitation of Christ. There are certain ways of abusing authority in which Jesus never indulged. The abbot likewise may not give himself permission to lose his self-control or treat his brothers with a highhandedness utterly alien to the Gospel.

If correction and challenge are an arduous part of the abbatial office, thank God there are moments that more than compensate for these difficulties. The abbot is the spiritual director of the community, and in great part this means that he is the minister of God's pardon. According to chapter 7 of the Rule, "On Humility," the monks ought to approach their abbot and confide their struggles and even their failings to him. Here it is not a question of the sacrament of confession, but rather an extension of the earlier desert monastic tradition of the "manifestation of thoughts." The monk opens his heart to the abbot, with its wounds and imperfections and sorrows. And how is the abbot to respond? The Rule says that the abbot's response should be the assurance of God's mercy, the communication of God's forgiveness. It is more than likely that the abbot himself has thought all the thoughts and experienced all the imperfections that his brethren are confiding to him (I can guarantee that this is true in my own case). This fact allows him to be "a merciful high priest," as Jesus is described in the Letter to the Hebrews (Heb 2:17). Christ could be limitlessly merciful without ever having sinned; the mercy of the abbot flows from a sharp consciousness of his own fragility as well as from the frequent blessed experience of having received the abundant pardon of God for his own offences.

The monk, like every Christian, is called to a certain kind of spiritual greatness. What stands between him and this high destiny is a lack of self-confidence or a failure to believe in the power of grace. Sometimes, therefore, it falls to the abbot to challenge a brother to go beyond his limits, if he discerns that the brother has potentialities that far exceed his present manner of monastic living. The abbot asks the monk to do the impossible (the Rule says he *orders* the monk to do the impossible). But this sense of impossibility is something subjective in the brother. The abbot has the grace to see that the brother will indeed be able to rise to the occasion, and that this breakthrough can permanently change his life for the better, in particular by releasing him from the paralysis of fear. The abbot's task is to communicate to the brother, "You can do it," or, in more theological language, "Nothing is impossible to God."

Last, and most important, the abbot is called to pray for the brothers. In many chapters of the second book of the *Dialogues* of Gregory the Great, "The Life and Miracles of Saint Benedict," the brothers manage to get into some difficulty or other and have to go looking for the abbot to resolve the situation. And where is he to be found? Usually in his monastic cell, already praying for just these brothers, eager to help them out of their difficult situation and already illumined through prayer with the beginning of a solution. Recently a holy monk said to me, "We poor human beings can't do much for each other, but we can always give witness, and we can always pray." The abbot is one who by his specific vocation is asked to be constantly interceding for his spiritual sons.

This chapter is about abbots, but if you remember the title, you've grasped that it is about any man who has the vocation to generate life—about every kind of father. All fatherhood is ultimately derived from the fatherhood of God. May all who participate in it receive the grace to be fathers after God's own heart.

Chapter Eleven. Separation from the World, Communion with the World

Abba Evagrius wrote in his treatise *On Prayer*, "The monk is someone who separates himself from all in order to be united to all" (#124). Like many of the Desert Fathers and later mystics, Evagrius made use of paradox in order to intensify his message, and to be able to verbalize it in as few words as possible: "separate in order to be united." But for us to arrive at a comprehension of what Evagrius wished to say so as to be able to put it into practice in some measure in our own lives, we will need more than a one-sentence commentary. We will need several chapters.

Let us begin by describing what it means concretely for a monk to separate himself from the world. First of all, at least in the Trappist, Camaldolese, and Carthusian traditions, separation from the world implies a certain geographical distance. Monasteries are built in deserts rather than in cities. The monk leaves the city behind to go out to a solitary place—even if he shares this solitude with other monks in a communitarian environment. For this reason, Christian monks have always looked to biblical figures such as Elijah and John the Baptist as their spiritual ancestors. These were men who lived apart from society, who took refuge in the desert. They had a mysterious intuition that the desert would be fruitful for them: that the desert would make them blossom spiritually and that they in turn would make the desert bloom.

Separation from the world as the ancient monks understood it—and as we continue to understand it today—is only possible if in addition to leaving the city behind, you also leave your possessions behind. If you take all the contents of your apartment with you into the monastic desert, you end up creating a resort instead of conforming yourself to the austere simplicity of the desert, which is by nature a place of the necessary rather than of the superfluous. When a candidate prepares to enter our monastery, there is a list of things to bring and a list of things not to bring, and the second list is much longer than first. Basically what the new monk can bring with him are the clothes he needs (apart from the monastic habit that will be given him), a small number of spiritual books, one or two religious images—a crucifix, an icon—and perhaps some photos of his family. And that's it. As we all know, objects—things—have a way of creating an ambience, generating an atmosphere. And when a monk drags into the monastery too many cherished, familiar things, he is really still living at home rather than emigrating to the new spiritual reality of the desert.

Most candidates don't find it too difficult to adapt themselves to this aspect of desert simplicity. They are not addicted to things. What is much more challenging is the separation from the world of persons, especially the near and dear ones. In the old days, this separation was much more radical than at present. But the contacts are still very limited in terms of writing to one's family (once a month in our case), telephone calls (only in emergency situations), emails (no), visits from the family (once a year). It is in this separation that one discovers how strong and close are the ties that bind us to our families, how much of our identity, our experience of ourselves, depends on our ongoing relationship with the members of our family.

Certainly there is no novice who doesn't question many times over, "What is the sense of all these restrictions? Why can't I call my mom once a week just to see how she is and to let her know I'm fine?" It takes time for the monk to acquire an intuition into the importance—the indispensability—of this separation in light of the goal he wishes to arrive at. And obviously, the middle period—the time between the goodbyes and the ability to intuitively understand and accept the separation—is painful. When young monks tell me that they miss their family and friends, I answer, "Thank God! If there weren't people out there that you missed, that would mean you were a person who had never learned to love. We wouldn't want that kind of person in the monastery." The young people look at me and scratch their heads. Perhaps they think that I am being as paradoxical as Evagrius.

There is still another dimension of separation from the world to be mentioned—one that really does isolate the monk from the world. It is the radical diminishment of contact with the media. The monastic desert has no televisions, no radios, no DVDs, no smartphones. Often there are few newspapers and very few magazines. The superior finds a way of communicating to the community the most important events of world and national news, so that the monks can lift up these situations to God in prayer. As I write this article, we are all praying especially for the peaceful resolution of the situation in Libya and for all the nations of the Moslem Middle East, passing through a period of profound and substantial political and cultural change. But there is an awful lot that we don't know about—not because we despise it, but because we need not to know in order to arrive at our inward destination. We are not quite at the point of another ancient desert monk who after fifty years of monastic life asked a rare visitor to his cell, "Does Alexandria still exist?" But we do understand what the nineteenth-century philosopher Henry Thoreau wished to say in his essay "Life without Principle," when he counseled, "Don't read the Times. Read the eternities."

What is the purpose of all this separation? Let me borrow a comparison made by the Swiss psychiatrist Carl Jung, one that he drew from the world of alchemy and applied to the world of psychotherapy. In the alchemical tradition, in order to carry out the great dream of transforming base metal into gold, it is necessary to put the metal into a container, seal it hermetically, and expose it to great heat. This *vas bene clausum* offers the only possibility of bringing about the transmutation of lead into gold. If air gets into the vessel or if the heat is not kept high and constant enough, the chemical change will not take place. Jung regarded the psychiatrist's office as the *vas bene clausum*. Only two persons were allowed to be there—therapist and patient. The environment was closed to every other person and every other influence. In this hot and stifling atmosphere—in this desert—it was possible that patients, through the intermediary of the analyst, could come to genuinely experience themselves in their truth and in consequence be radically changed—become gold (*Psychology and Alchemy*).

Separation from the world in the monastic context, as described above, can be understood in this way. The passage from the city to the desert is the voluntary entry into the vessel and the sealing of the lid. It is something like the descent of Alice into the rabbit hole or the descent of many heroes of antiquity into the underworld. Here, where everything distracting is taken away, where the comforts and amusements of the world disappear, people can come to meet themselves, perhaps for the first time. That is the hope. And obviously, the other person in the consulting room is God. His presence, his holiness, his truth, provide the heat. In this fiery furnace, the new self can be formed—the person who is wholly separated—wholly individuated—and totally in communion.

Chapter Twelve. Self-Knowledge

What is it that happens to the monk when he separates himself from the world? He becomes aware of his own thoughts. It is not that he begins to think radically new or different thoughts, but simply that, like it or not, he begins to be conscious—acutely conscious—of what he has been thinking for many years.

Thoughts, in the monastic vocabulary, do not refer to each and every formulation of an idea that passes through the mind. They do not have to do with information or with the rational processing of data. The thoughts of which the early monastic fathers and mothers are speaking are "suggestions" that present themselves to our consciousness in a forceful, and even passionate, manner. They are repetitive, insistent, demanding, even obsessive. And they wish to push us towards a decision, either internal or external: internal as a consent of the will to what the suggestion presents to our mind, external as putting into practice the act that the suggestion proposes. In a non-monastic context, the term that would come closest to this understanding of a thought would be *temptation*. But the monastic tradition prefers to call them (in Greek, the language of early Christian monastic theology) *logismoi*—thoughts laden with passion.

It is not easy to come into conscious contact with these thoughts, although they are constantly arising within us and acting upon us. This difficulty has several causes. In the first place, the content of these thoughts generally represents that which we would prefer *not* to think, *not* to want, *not* to do, *not* to be. The *logismoi* are always humiliating, because they reveal to us a whole world of impulses to which we are ashamed to be subject. There is no such thing as a *logismos* towards generosity, courage, self-sacrifice. Certainly, with the grace of the Holy Spirit we are capable of having noble ideas and realizing them as well. But in this case we are speaking of inspiration from above, and not of the insidious suggestions that push us towards what is base, self-centered, or vindictive. The *logismoi* tend to remain hidden, because as long as they remain concealed, we can think much more positively about ourselves. Hidden *logismoi* are good for maintaining a positive self-image. The problem with this, however, is that the person never truly comes to know himself. He knows a part of himself—the easier part, the sweeter part. But he does not know the whole story.

A second cause for the concealment of the *logismoi* is that their power over us increases in direct proportion to their ability to escape our awareness. They work best and most effectively in the dark, in the dark of what today we call the unconscious. When they are lifted into the conscious part of ourselves, they lose much of their attractive force. Once in the conscious sphere, they are exposed to such fundamental elements of our spiritual make-up as our free will, our capacity to reflect and evaluate, our basic moral values. This simple contact always weakens them and many times defeats them. If, however, they can isolate themselves from our liberty, our rationality, and our morality, they have much more of a free hand. And the *logismoi*, like everything else that lives, have a survival instinct. So they generally prefer to hide out in the basement, where they can continue to flourish and to influence us without our knowing it.

The third reason for the ability of the *logismoi* to function unperceived is that for the person who does not put up any resistance to them, their activity is tranquil and unobtrusive. In the person accustomed to give in to the suggestions of the *logismoi*, the *logismoi* have become habitual to the point of appearing normal. Saint Ignatius of Loyola, who dedicated much of his spiritual reflection to the diverse inner movements within the soul, affirms in his *Spiritual Exercises* that the person dominated by his *logismoi* experiences their onslaught as nothing more violent than a drop of water gently falling onto a sponge. Once in a while he might experience a so-called twinge of conscience, but this will generally not be enough to make him take a stand against them. Those readers who have read Tolstoy's *Anna Karenina* will identify in the character of Stephen Oblonsky a person completely—and pacifically—surrendered to the allurements of his *logismoi*.

The *logismoi* are the very atmosphere of the world—the world in the sense of the dominant, secular culture, whether that culture be that of imperial Rome, medieval Florence, or contemporary São Paulo. The *logismoi* are the value system of the world insofar as it is alienated from God. This understanding gives us an insight into another aspect of the separation from the world that we discussed in the last chapter. When the monk separates himself from the world, he is doing something much more radical than changing addresses from city to desert. He is proclaiming that he will no longer live according to the predominant *logismoi*. Instead, he will take up a *logomachia*—a battle against the suggestions that the *logismoi* continually offer him (like so many courtiers, in the image of Saint Augustine). Rather than consenting to their insinuations, he will resist them by constantly counter-proposing a word of the Scriptures. As Saint Benedict says, he will "dash them against the rock of Christ"—the rock of the gospels (RB 4.50).

The monk who has just joined the monastery does not really know very much about the *logismoi* from first-hand experience, although usually he has read a fair amount about them, in the writings of the first great monastic theologians of the fourth and fifth centuries, Evagrius and his disciple John Cassian. It would be good at this point to name the *logismoi* and to situate them in their three fundamental groups. Simply identifying them represents a first step in freeing ourselves from their control.

Perhaps it will come as a surprise to us that we are already familiar with the list of *logismoi*, or rather, with an adaptation of the list made in the sixth century by Pope Saint Gregory the Great. He took the eight "thoughts" and slightly condensed them into seven items that he called "capital sins." In Gregory's version the seven capital sins are gluttony, lust, avarice, anger, sloth, envy, and pride. In Evagrius's original formulation, in place of sloth there are two *logismoi*: sadness and *acedia*. (*Acedia* is a characteristically monastic experience, and we will have occasion to return to it later.) What is really different in the conceptions of Evagrius and Gregory is that for Gregory, these realities are immediately named *sins*—things consented to or acted upon—whereas for the monk, they are *thoughts*—possibilities, to which the monk might give in with greater or lesser frequency (hopefully lesser, the more he perseveres in his ascetic endeavor) but which he desires to resist and, if possible, with God's grace eventually overcome.

For the monk who lives with them day and night, it is imperative that he recognize the *logismoi*, at least in their initial assault, as simple possibilities with no implication of sin. For at certain epochs of his life, the cycle of suggestion, awareness, resistance, and rejection of the *logismoi* will be the dominant activity of the monk's life—his "inner work" as it is sometimes called. And it is an arduous inner work, this ongoing vigilance and combat and prayer to Christ to overcome suggestions that are in no way compatible with the Gospel. It assimilates the monk to Jesus in his forty days in the desert, one of the mysteries of our Lord's life most intimately associated with the monastic vocation.

The *logismoi* fall into three groups, according to the three aspects of the human person that they seek to deform. There are the *logismoi* of our bodiliness, our physicality: gluttony, lust, and avarice; the *logismoi* of our affectivity: anger, sadness, and *acedia*; and the *logismoi* of our rationality: vanity and pride.

How these *logismoi* attack the monk and how he fights back will be the theme of the next chapter. Because the *logismoi* afflict not only monks but all human persons, it will be a blessing for all of us to come in touch with a tradition that has developed a method of facing them and becoming free from their oppression.

Chapter Thirteen. Manifestation of Thoughts: The Spiritual Director

According to Saint Bernard, the *logismoi* of which we have been speaking ought to be recognized above all as "suggestions." *Someone* is proposing a thought to us, is recommending an inner attitude or an outward course of action. This "someone" can easily be ourselves, and according to Evagrius, in the majority of cases the suggestion does indeed come from ourselves. All of us spend a lot of time talking to ourselves! This is one of the most normal and universal activities of humanity, and it is often quite harmless, although that does not necessarily mean that we should also follow our own suggestions. When these proceed from our own interiority, according to Evagrius, they ought to be evaluated a little further, in accord with their consonance with the Gospel and the norms of prudence.

But it is important to be aware that there are two other possible sources of suggestions: the good Spirit—that is to say, the Holy Spirit—and the evil spirit, the devil. In the case of suggestions from the good spirit, we ought immediately to accept them and put them into practice. When the suggestions come from the evil spirit, we should give them absolutely no quarter, but reject them out of hand. The difficulty is that it is not always so easy to discern what is the source of a particular suggestion—not so simple to know who is on the other side of the line of our inner telephone. Just as in the world of contemporary virtual communication, so in the world of our thoughts, there are persons pretending to be somebody they are not, with the idea of making us buy their product—be that product a personal decision that will affect our lives or a non-existent object ordered through the Internet. (I have personally bought a number of theological books online that never arrived because they were never written in the first place.) As Saint Paul already recognized in his Second Letter to the Corinthians, "Satan can disguise himself as an angel of light" (2 Cor 11:14).

The key word for deciding on the acceptance, rejection, or further evaluation of thoughts is precisely *discernment*—the ability to penetrate to the origin of a particular suggestion, name its source, and respond to it appropriately. This is tremendously important for all of us, monks or not, because all of us live bombarded by an immense number of thoughts. Mental and emotional possibilities present themselves to us all day (and all night) long, and as human persons we cannot simply be passive victims of this onslaught or neutral observers of the great and multi-colored variety of material that presents itself to our heart and our mind. We have the responsibility—and thank God the capacity as well— to freely choose the right response to every one of the suggestions that appears on our inner screen. However, in order to be able to live this reality successfully, we have to develop the knack for identifying the spiritual origin of each one of the suggestions that present themselves to us. In very large measure, the mental tiredness and confusion that so many people experience today are due not to bad will but to an inability to see beyond the surface of their thoughts into their real source and their real implications. When this is the case, life literally turns into one big headache.

How can we learn to discern our thoughts—become aware of them, evaluate them, and deal appropriately with them? First of all, there are some things we can do on our own. We can cultivate an attitude of attentiveness; we can accompany our own mental activity. For instance, in accord with the teaching of the desert monks, we can train ourselves to notice what *thoughts* are presenting themselves to us with an unusual degree of frequency. Just as a dream that repeats itself is sure to be psychologically significant by the mere fact of its repetition, so a thought that keeps coming back to us is sure to be important by its very insistence in knocking at the doors of our mind. As a matter of fact, every pattern is important. Whatever keeps coming back to us has a message to deliver. Along with noting the frequency of a particular thought, we can also learn to be aware of its affective impact. Thoughts that pass through our minds like a bird passing through the sky and leaving no track do not require much attention, because their effect is momentary. They engage neither our reason nor our will. On the other hand, thoughts that perturb us, thoughts that have strong emotional repercussions: these demand some sort of treatment. A thought that frightens, saddens, angers, or exhilarates us is a notable thought. It is exactly the kind of thought that I ask my monks to record in their notebook (written or not) in order to bring up and reflect about in our next session of spiritual direction.

And this brings us to a central point. In the end, learning to deal with the immensely rich world of our thoughts, and in particular our passionate thoughts, is not a solitary project. It is a duet. We acquire the ability to discern and decide about our thoughts by working together with a spiritual director, someone to whom we can confidently manifest what's going on in our inner world.

What is gained by the manifestation of thoughts? A lot depends on the spiritual maturity of the person to whom we open ourselves. The monastic tradition forcefully asserts that passionate thoughts should only be presented to someone who has attained the state that is called passionlessness (in Greek, *apatheia*). *Apatheia* is the state of soul of someone who through long and arduous inner work with himself and in collaboration with his own "elder" has truly become free of the pressures of the passions. This does not mean that he no longer experiences the appearance of the whole range of human thoughts, but that he has attained a persistent tranquility in the face of any and all of them. Thoughts of violence, of lust, of hatred, of despair may still present themselves to him. But he has learned to respond to all of them in perfect peace.

The indwelling presence of the Holy Spirit has become so decisive in him that nothing that diverges from the Holy Spirit can exert any influence over him, either to attract him or to frighten him. When I was named novice master of my first monastic community in the United States thirty-two years ago, I was presented with a marvelous pen and ink drawing of Saint Anthony, the father of Christian monasticism. In this drawing, he is shown seated in the desert, surrounded by all the imaginable monsters of thought: pictorial representations of all the strange and powerful and dangerous realities that are capable of rising up in the human heart. The artwork shows them in the form of animals: lions, tigers, bears, serpents, and savage birds. All of them stretch out their paws, their claws, their wings, their teeth to attack him. They come close, but they never succeed in touching him. And Anthony's face is totally serene, imperturbably peaceful. The passions no longer have any power over him.

Exactly because of his own spiritual liberty, the elder has power to effectively help others in the battle of thoughts. His mind is a spotless mirror, and the thoughts of those who come to him for advice will be projected onto his intellect, clearly and integrally. The disciple sees his own thoughts in a very partial and unsatisfactory way—hazily and distortedly—because he is still the victim of rationalization and of unacknowledged desires. The master immediately grasps them for what they are. No longer duped by the wiles of the passions in his own inner life, he is immune to being tricked by them as they show up in the lives of those who seek his counsel.

But is it enough for the spiritual director to have a clear-sighted perception of the thoughts of the person he accompanies? Obviously not. It is simply a first, indispensable step. For only if the master sees with clarity what is going on inside the disciple can the disciple be brought to a liberating truth about his affective and moral reality. (By the way, according to the tradition, there are monastic elders capable of discerning the inner state of a disciple without needing to be told verbally. They possess the gift of *cardiognosia*, the "knowledge of hearts." We are familiar with this gift from the gospels, where the text frequently reads, "And Jesus, knowing their thoughts, said. . . .") What needs to happen next is a living transfer of the master's knowledge to the disciple, not simply as information, not simply as a hard copy, but as an increasing capacity on the part of the disciple to accurately read himself by himself, and with the wisdom to perceive how to use this knowledge in a way that brings him to a stable peace. The goal is to attain that equanimity that the monastic tradition describes as *semper idem,* "always the same," that emotional dependability that we often see in the faces of statues of the Buddha, and above all that we see in the person of Jesus in the Gospel. How this transfer takes place will be the theme of the following chapter.

Chapter Fourteen.
The Transmission of Freedom

Abba Evagrius once wrote that with the passage of time, the relationship between spiritual director and the young monk gradually changes from one of authority and obedience to one of equality: both master and disciple become "gods in the one God" (*Centuries* IV, 58). This is because the director's intention is to transmit his wisdom in a living and effective way, to enable the disciple to rule himself (in Greek, "to attain *autarchia*") in direct dependence on the Holy Spirit rather than on another human person. The director's dearest wish is to become disposable, to no longer be needed by the disciple, who has now achieved freedom from the passions and the capacity to see and act in truth for himself. How does the director go about doing this? How does he help the beginner gradually to come to that immediate and lasting contact with the Holy Spirit who "teaches us all things," who "guides us into all truth" (see John 14:26; 16:13)?

Freedom from the passions, illumination by the Spirit. What is the director's *modus agendi* for bringing this about in the life of his disciple? Clearly, the most basic prerequisite is for the director to recognize that such a transformation will not be his own work as a spiritual health-care professional, but rather will be a work of the Divine Spirit with which he will attempt to collaborate. On the one hand, this collaboration will consist in his communicating insights and practices from the monastic tradition to the disciple, on the other—more important—in his personally incarnating God's love and commitment to him.

Let us begin with the insights and practices. The first and simplest is to let the disciple learn by experience that often enough simply revealing a *logismos* suffices to bring about a liberation from an obsessive thought or a compulsive behavior. Cassian, the chief transmitter of Evagrian thinking to the Occidental church, tells a story in Book V of the *Institutes* of a young fourth-century Coptic monk who had the habit of stealing food from the monastery dispensary—understandable enough when we remember that the monastic diet of the epoch was two small rolls, a pinch of salt, and water. The young monk was ashamed of his thefts but unable to put an end to them. One evening his elder, aware of the whole situation, managed to steer the conversation around to the subject of food and how tempting it could be to anyone to nab something extra for himself every once in a while. The young monk, filled with repentance, declared that he himself fell into just that category. Immediately, to his own amazement, he discovered that the desire had simply gone. Being honest in the presence of another had produced a long-desired transformation. Humility brings unexpected freedom.

A second point of practical formation is aiding the disciple to "accompany his own thoughts." Through the practice of exterior and interior silence, we can move beyond having thoughts and feelings that affect us or even control us without our being truly aware of them or capable of responding to them, to a state where we habitually observe them as they arise within us and freely choose those we wish to accept and those we wish to reject. There is a whole school of monastic spirituality founded on the practice of *nepsis*—vigilance—the continual awareness of what is happening to us interiorly and the tranquil process of separating the productive from the destructive. We are not obliged to give in to every passionate thought just because it comes our way. Having seen it from far off and identified it as prejudicial, we are free to say, "No, thank you."

Sometimes this "No, thank you" is not too well received. Passionate thoughts can be insistent; they want to have their way. In this case, the master can pass on a third practice to the disciple, known as *logomachia*, literally, "the battle of thoughts." *Logomachia* simply requires opposing a holy and constructive thought to a thought about to lead us down a dark and dangerous alley. Where do these holy thoughts come from? Above all, from the Scriptures.

The Scriptures are a mine of thoughts endowed with the wisdom of God and the power of God. They are, as we daily proclaim in the liturgy, "the word of the Lord," and their origin in him makes them effective weapons in the hour of temptation. Many ancient writers recommend creating an inner file of such Scripture texts, appropriate for different occasions: texts that help us liberate ourselves from anxiety or envy or sadness or anger. Saint Benedict in the Prologue of his Rule speaks in a more generic way and advises monks to "dash all these thoughts, while they are still young, against the rock of Christ" (RB Prol. 28). He is probably referring to the invocation of the name of Christ as a universal weapon against harmful thoughts.

Many of us Western Christians are aware that for centuries Eastern monks have practiced what is called the "Jesus prayer"—the inner calling to mind of the name of Jesus, either by itself or as part of a formula, such as, "Lord Jesus Christ, Son of God, have mercy on me a sinner." Intended as a means of creating greater intimacy with the Lord, it has always been used as well to "extinguish the fiery darts of the Evil One" (Eph 6:16). (By the way, the part of chapter six from Paul's Letter to the Ephesians from which this quotation is drawn [6:10-17] is in itself a small treatise on *logomachia*.)

Another practical help that the director can render is to enable a young monk to identify his personal vulnerabilities. Saint Ignatius of Loyola says that each of us has aspects of character that are more susceptible than others to being stirred up. One person suffers from a poor self-image; another is prone to irritability; a third is convinced that nobody likes him. Ignatius compares the Evil One to a clever general always on the lookout for a breach in a Christian's defenses. If he can enter there, the whole citadel of the person becomes accessible to him. The director thus seeks to sensitize the person he accompanies to the nature of his particular weakness and to make him especially careful to examine himself when a passionate thought arises from that aspect of his personality.

Beyond all these practices (and the examples I have given are by no means exhaustive), there is the more profound reality of the director's provisionally taking the place of God. Remember the quotation from Evagrius at the beginning of this chapter, "gods in the one God"? Well, the starting-point for arriving at this joyful conclusion is that the director alone be like a god in the one God. By this I mean that it is absolutely crucial that all through this long, tiring, and painful process of liberation from the passions that the disciple is going through, the director steadily let him know, or rather experience, what God feels in his regard. For God is immensely moved by all this fidelity on the disciple's part, all his hard work to overcome the impediments to a fullness of friendship between God and himself. God already loves this seeker, this striver, infinitely—and the fact that this young man or woman is responding wholeheartedly to God's love stirs God profoundly.

God of course is used to loving—that is his essence, his definition. When someone loves him back, he may not be surprised, but he is certainly touched, and touched in his core. The director, by his patience with the disciple, by his compassion with him throughout his struggles, by his unshakable peace throughout all this transforming work that is going on, has to make palpable to the disciple the abiding and unshakable love God has for him. Why? First of all, because the disciple cannot go through this upheaval unless he experiences the tenderness of God, which he still requires a human face to perceive. And second, because it is true. Trustworthy, unshakable love is what God really feels for his struggling creature. If the director can communicate this, the disciple will become free.

Chapter Fifteen.
Humility and Confidence

Among the myriad stories of elders and their disciples in the *Lives of the Desert Fathers*, one is particularly striking. It tells of a young disciple with a very strong sexual urge. Many were the times that he gave in to temptation, though never without some initial attempt at resistance. Yet fight as he would, he was more often conquered than conqueror. As it happened, he died before his spiritual father, and the elder prayed earnestly for his soul, doubtful about his eternal destiny. One night, however, shortly after the disciple's passing away, the old monk had a powerful experience in prayer. He saw heaven thrown open and a myriad of angels in jubilation, waiting to receive a soul into the habitations of the blessed. "Whose victory am I witnessing?" the old monk asked himself. "How great the monk must be who is being welcomed with such joy by the angels of God!" When, squinting and stretching his neck, the ancient was finally able to identify who it was receiving the crown of glory, he was not only surprised. He was shocked. He was not only shocked, he was scandalized. It was his young disciple—*that* one. Out of a sense of duty, he felt impelled to raise an objection. Catching the eye of one of the angels, he said, "But don't you know who that is whom you're crowning? Don't you know what he *did*!" The angel, with the meekness and the tranquility proper to the citizens of heaven, replied, "Yes, I know. But I also know that every morning he sincerely asked pardon of God, did what he could to avoid occasions of sin, and trusted in God's mercy. That is why he is entering into such great glory."

In the last few chapters, we have seen that growth in self-knowledge, particularly through the relationship with a spiritual master, can lead to *autarchia*, dominion over one's interior movements, and in some cases bring a person to *apatheia*—a freedom from the passions. That is *one* of its fruits. But it is not the only one, and it is not a guaranteed one. The young monk of the apothegm I just recounted is not an isolated case, an inexplicable exception. There are many people—religious and lay alike—who struggle their whole lives against sadness, anger, lust, and sloth without definitively winning the battle.

Or rather, without winning it in this way. For there is a fruit of the battle against the passions and the deepening self-knowledge that comes with it that is available to all of us, if we are willing to receive it. That fruit is humility. Humility is the conviction, attained at great cost, through much experience and by a mixture of wins and losses, that we are not exactly the person we would like to be, nor will we ever be that person in this life. We are who we are, warts and all, and it is the acceptance of ourselves without airbrushing and self-deception that leads us to humility. As the years go by, as we pass from being young monks to not-so-young monks to old monks (or nuns or bishops or politicians), and as we continue to keep an eye on ourselves, we discover that struggle though we may, we continue to fall, sometimes often, sometimes badly, just as we did in the early days.

But now we contemplate this unfortunately unchanging reality of ourselves without excuses. We don't put the blame for our irritability on another person, on our upbringing (who has ever had the perfect parents that he or she deserved?), or on our circumstances. We simply see with clarity that this is how we are. I will never forget how moved I was by an elderly monk coming to me many years ago and saying with the utmost simplicity, "Father, please help me. I have a problem with anger." I waited for him to count off the mitigating factors—why it wasn't his fault, whose fault it really was—but he said no more. He had told the truth about himself—he had a problem with anger—and he came to me precisely to speak the truth and to ask if there was some way that I could help him in his affliction. *That* was humility.

But how is it that people can accept themselves in this way? How can they accept failure? Where do they get the courage to admit to themselves that years of serious struggling against one or another vice have brought them only a little further along—if that!—on the path of virtue? That is an insightful question, and the answer is that by itself humbling self-knowledge is intolerable. It can only be tolerated, and even welcomed, when it is joined to another virtue, a virtue that is one of the greatest of Christian blessings: confidence. We can even say that it is only as self-knowledge is joined to confidence that it really becomes humility.

I remember hearing in a talk given by my abbot when I was a novice that, "A monastery is a place where we learn the value of failure." The remark was purposely paradoxical, and all the more so for a novice in search of the heights of doctrine and virtue that Saint Benedict's Rule speaks about. Now I realize that for the older monks the abbot's assertion was a familiar item in their own personal stock of wisdom. Failure in the monastery is precious because it drives us to God. Initially it drives us to him in fear, in frustration, in resentment: "How could you have allowed this to happen to me who serve you day and night?" "What's the good of depriving myself of x, y, and z in the monastery if the results are going to be no better than they were out in the world?" "Do you hate me? Do I have to leave the Eden of the monastery now that I have sinned, as Adam and Eve had to leave Paradise after their sin?"

But if we keep talking to God, we come to experience something utterly unexpected (at least, the first time that it happens): we feel his hand, as it were, gently raising our downcast and tearstained face to look into his face. And what do we discover in his face? Not fury, not disappointment, not rejection. We see compassion for the pain we are suffering, we see appreciation for the efforts that we are making out of the desire to please him, and above all we see loving acceptance—pardon that is more than pardon, pardon that is an embrace. In Bernard Shaw's play *Saint Joan*, the saint said that she heard the voice of God in the church bells. "And what do the church bells say?" she was asked. "Be brave, go on. I am your help. God will save France." To all of us, French or not, God speaks in the same deep comforting tones of the church bells. "I know. I understand. I love." God is not saying that sin is wonderful. In fact, God is not talking about sin at all. He is talking about love, his age-old love, deeper and stronger and realer than all other things. It is this that he offers us at the moment of failure when we are forced to know ourselves in a way we would prefer not to. If we can keep quiet at these moments and let him speak, he will assure us that our transgression has not ruptured the relationship with him—that *no* transgression can rupture the relationship. Passing through this same experience again and again, we will gradually come to believe that God means what he is saying, and we will gradually come to believe *him*. *That* is confidence.

Guerric of Igny, one of Saint Bernard's disciples and later an abbot himself, left behind only one work—a collection of sermons for the liturgical year. In one of them, he writes that we go to heaven falling and rising, falling and rising, falling and rising. It doesn't matter that we fall and rise. What matters is that we are going to our heavenly homeland. By far, one of the best things about coming to know ourselves is that it pushes us to know God better, and more truly. A humble person can pray with all the assurance of personal knowledge the words of Psalm 136, "His love endures forever."

Chapter Sixteen. Compassion

In his treatise on the common life, Baldwin of Forde, another of the monastic theologians of the twelfth century, wrote that we Christians are sharers in a threefold communion: a communion in misery, a communion in grace, and a communion in glory.

What does it mean to have a communion in misery? It means that if we allow ourselves to know our poverty and failure, not becoming embittered by this knowledge but discovering in it a greater motive for putting our trust in God, this will change not only our relationship with ourselves and our relationship with him; it will also transform our relationship with our neighbor.

As long as we deny our moral and spiritual limitations, or as long as they cause us a destructive shame, every other human person is a source of irritation. Mysteriously, each contact with another brings us in touch with the unresolved conflict between the person we want to be and the person we are. This is a tremendously uncomfortable feeling, and we do what we can to feel something different. We look away from the pain of our doubleness (who we want to be and who we really are), and we fix our gaze on our neighbor, to find some relief in this distraction. And what do we discover? Either that as a matter of fact he is even worse than we are—what joy!—or that he is not as bad as we are—what a shame! Given the fact that we were made for joy and not for sorrow, it seems to be in our best interests to see the neighbor as more sinful, more defective than we ourselves. Thus the joy grows: out of thirty-five people in this community, I am fundamentally better than thirty-two of them (and the other two probably have problems that I haven't yet discovered). Only this kind of joy is not very healthy—the aftertaste is absolutely horrible—and it certainly is not the kind of joy God had in mind when he created us for happiness.

At any rate, we can see that this kind of relationship is in fact anything but a relationship. I am not open to the identity, the reality, of the other. In himself, he does not interest me in the least. He is purely functional; he helps me deal with my difficult feelings about myself—alleviating them, if I can prove him a greater sinner than I am, exacerbating them if I have to admit that despite all my efforts, he really is a gentleman and a scholar.

By the way, I have robbed this line of thinking from Saint Bernard in his splendid treatise on the *Steps of Humility and Pride*. I don't feel too bad about this robbery, however, because Bernard himself was a well-known thief from patristic sources: Origen, Augustine, Gregory the Great. See what I've just done? I said, "I might be bad, but St. Bernard was worse." This process of negative comparison is almost irresistible!

Humility, says Saint Bernard, is attained by reversing the direction of our thoughts. Instead of attempting to resolve the conflict between the ideal and real self by hurtful comparison with the neighbor, the true solution is to withdraw into our own selves—abide with ourselves for a while, in order to come to a good, clear appreciation of who we are. The Latin monastic fathers called this practice of introversion *habitare secum*—living with oneself. We might call it learning to put up with ourselves, with the commitment of accepting whatever it is that we discover by entering into our inner hermitage.

Obviously, not everything we encounter within will be beautiful. The last few chapters have made this clear. It was precisely this impossible wish to be immaculate that we renounced by going into the inner hermitage. Now that we are there, the trick is to sweat it out: to persevere in seeing what we see—without any tinkering or trickery. Bernard says that doubtlessly this perseverance will be the source of many tears—tears of regret, tears of repentance, tears of the loss of our illusions about ourselves—but in the long run it will also be a source of profound peace. "Blessed are they who mourn, for they will be consoled" (Matt 5:4). How interesting this beatitude is—it doesn't say that we will console ourselves or that we will find some consolation for ourselves. It says, using the passive voice, that someone other than us will console us.

This someone, as we have seen, is God himself, the Father of mercies and the God of all consolation, as Paul calls him in the opening passage of his Second Letter to the Corinthians. All these elements—tears of self-knowledge, repentance, and the experience of being consoled by God—are indispensable if we are ever to embark on the spiritual life. When I was novice master in my monastery in Massachusetts, the abbot regularly asked about one or another novice, "Has he had a good cry yet?" If I said, "Yes," the abbot responded, "Great," and I could see that he felt confident of a positive outcome for the struggling beginner. If I said, "No," his face became serious, and he said, "Let's pray that God give him this grace in the near future." By the way, Saint Bernard calls this conjunction of self-knowledge, repentance, consolation by God, and inner peace "the first kiss" (*On the Song of Songs* 3). For him, it is the first genuine mystical experience: to know oneself as one is and to know that same self as loved by God.

"We are at peace with God through our Lord Jesus Christ" (Rom 5:1). When we have come to be truly at peace with God and at peace with ourselves because of his acceptance of us in Christ, everything changes. The journey out of the inner hermitage is very different from the journey in. We entered almost in spite of ourselves and annoyed with the world; we go out smiling, and in search of brothers and sisters. When the door of the cell of self-knowledge swings open through a profound experience of the mercy of God, we are convinced that, returning to the outside world, we are going to find brothers and sisters—a multitude of them, as Saint Paul says.

Nor are we disappointed in our hope. It is not that the world has passed through a cosmic purification while we were in the hermitage. It is not that everyone has overcome the defects that we previously contemplated with the most intense and pitiless clarity, as well as with a good dose of irritation. The people are just the same as they were before—except for the fact that now they are lovable. How are they lovable? Have we who were so clear-sighted before, so on the mark, lost all our criteria of evaluation? No; we have simply laid them aside, at least for the time being. We have discovered something much more important about all the people who surround us—they are just like us. All striving, all falling, all struggling to rise again. All trying to break out of the net of narcissism, all making heroic efforts that are sometimes successful and other times not. "Incredible!" we exclaim. "They are just like us!" And we are overcome with a wave of tenderness for them—for their good intentions, their good efforts, their limitations, even their sins that they are not yet able to leave behind. Tenderness and loving pity—this is what we feel for them, and we probably don't even realize that what we are experiencing is the overflow, the passing on, of the tenderness and loving pity that God feels for *us*.

The good priest in the confessional listening to the penitent, the good spiritual director attending to his directee (why doesn't English have a better word for this?), the good parent listening to his child confess a childish misdemeanor, spontaneously feels how alike and not how different the two of them are. "How much we need the mercy of God," they think. "How wonderful it is that we have it—that we have it together." The church is the community of those who thankfully experience the mercy of God together. This is what Baldwin meant when he spoke of a "communion in misery." And now we see that it is a holy communion.

Chapter Seventeen.
To Love as God Loves

If you took the compassion and tenderness that we have been speaking about, raised it to the nth power, and gave it to a monk as a present, you would be giving him his heart's desire. What would be the name of that present? To love as God loves. However much a monk desires to become a man of prayer, prayer—even mystical prayer—is a only a means for him. Divine love is the goal.

Is it possible to arrive at such an amazingly exalted goal? (By the way, that this really was the goal of the desert monks is beautifully demonstrated in a book about them with just this title, *To Love as God Loves*, written by the patristics scholar Roberta Bondi.[1]) Perhaps it is what Karl Rahner called an "asymptotic goal"—the vertical line to which a geometric curve approaches ever more closely without ever actually touching it. Or perhaps it is better than that. The Cistercian fathers of the twelfth century wrote frequently of "unity of spirit," being one spirit with God's Spirit. Now God's Spirit *is* divine love, and if that unity of spirit was more than a dream of these twelfth-century monks but rather their actual experience, who knows if it could not be our own experience as well? How often we Catholics used to pray, "Jesus, meek and humble of heart, make my heart like unto thine"! What if Jesus actually heard and accepted this prayer and set about conforming our heart more and more to his divine-human heart

---

[1] Roberta C. Bondi, *To Love As God Loves: Conversations With the Early Church* (Minneapolis: Fortress Press, 1984).

until he succeeded in producing a perfect likeness? Then indeed, when we loved, we would love as God loves. The idea takes our breath away a little—and it should.

Let's begin a little more humbly and look at some of the milestones in this growth towards divine love, asymptotic or not. I think that the first indication that we are heading in the right direction would be what the Jesuits call the "plus sign": "Giving someone the plus sign," as they say. This practice comes from the *Spiritual Exercises* of Saint Ignatius, where he counsels the person making the exercises always to give the most positive interpretation possible to the other person's gestures, words, and deeds. It is not a question of calling evil good, of being intellectually dishonest. Instead, it is a recognition that every human word and act is open to a very wide gamut of interpretation, depending not so much on the objective quality of that word or act but upon the inner attitude with which we observe and judge it. The Desert Fathers likewise knew that distrust and hypercriticalness were typical of the sinful human person, and they too did all they could to counteract it.

Both Ignatius and the Desert Fathers are questioning us: "Who knows if the great majority of your neighbor's deeds upon which you habitually sit in judgment are not in fact good deeds, which you read incorrectly, because of the way you look at them, because of the ugly heart with which you look at them?" Ignatius and the Desert Fathers remind us to go back to the Sermon on the Mount (we can never go back often enough) and to learn again to take the plank out of our own eye so that we will be able to see accurately if there is a speck in our brother's eye. By the way, even if there *were* a speck, a speck is not such a very large thing. It does very little harm and would not be noticed at all by us, unless we were studying our brother's conduct under a microscope. The plus sign is the initial step to universal love—divine love is always universal. A more formal name for it would be *benevolence*.

This is a beautiful and immensely optimistic theme—loving as God loves. As I write, I see that one chapter is not going to be sufficient for treating it. I consider that my good fortune, since simply thinking about the possibility of such love in the human person, for you the reader and for me the writer, is a source of joy.

On to the second step in our pilgrimage of love. I think we could call it *disponibility*—putting ourselves at the disposal of others. Not only our possessions, but our energy, our emotional resources and our time. The great rabbi of the generation before Jesus, Hillel, stated that whereas the affirmation "What's mine is mine and what's yours is yours" is justice, and the affirmation "What's mine is mine and what's yours is mine" is the sign of a depraved character, there exists a third possibility: "What's mine is yours and what's yours is yours."[2] This is the quality of charity of the saint, of the person who agrees with the saying of Jesus, "There is more joy in giving than in receiving." Various Desert Father stories tell of a monk being awakened from sleep by the presence of a thief who is systematically removing all the contents of his cell. According to the stories, the thief, anxious to get away unperceived—so he thinks—usually ends up missing some small treasure and heads out the door of the cell without it, to make his escape. What does the monk do? He calls after the thief—no, he *runs* after the thief with the missed object in his hands, pressing it upon the robber. "Wait! You almost lost the gem of the collection."

There is, obviously, something humorous in these accounts, and obviously they are a teaching on detachment and inner liberty. But this liberty is not a free-standing item; it exists in the service of charity. The monk actually *loves* the intruder (who is there that such a monk *doesn't* love?) and wants to give him, freely and joyfully, the best he has to offer. Never in such a story do we read of a monk thrashing in his bed as he watches the thief at work, struggling with himself to summon up the virtue to hand over to the thief even the objects that he would have left behind. No, the loving monk has what Jesus describes in the gospel as a "good and generous heart that produces a hundredfold," and it is his pleasure to give the thief all that he has. This is what we can't get our heads around: that the monk considers the thief his friend, believing as he does that all human beings, made in the image and likeness of God, are his friends. He no longer calls

[2] Charles Taylor, *Pirkei Avot: Sayings of the Jewish Fathers* (North Charleston, SC: CreateSpace Independent Publishing Platform, 2014), 5.

anyone his servants, but his friends. What wouldn't we give to have space in our heads for this attitude of the desert monks, so that we could live in spiritual friendship with all our fellow men and women?

With regard to making our time available for others—and time is always such a very precious commodity in the monastery where there are so many tasks to be done and so little opportunity for the reading, praying, and just being that so attract the monastic personality—we have the beautiful example of the nineteenth-century Russian monk, Saint Seraphim of Sarov. Whenever any-one came to visit him in his cell to consult him on a spiritual question—and there was always an immense line of people wait-ing, almost from one side of Russia to the other (Seraphim was the Curé of Ars, the Padre Pio of his own time and place)—he invariably greeted them with the same phrase, which was more sung than spoken, "Welcome, my joy!" *This* really is love—to consider every person who knocks at the door of one's life, even before we know him, as our joy, and to close the book we were reading or leave off the letter we were writing so that we can immediately dedicate our entire attention to the new arrival. And to do it with a smile, because the neediness of the person who has come to us will begin to be healed by the smile of welcome, and because the smile promises, "All will be well. We are here together, you and I, surrounded by the grace of the humble and victorious Christ who is watching over us and who makes all things turn out for the good of those who love him."

You see, I was right. The theme is bigger than the space of a chapter. We will continue it in the following one—if that's ok with you, my joy.

Chapter Eighteen. To Love as God Loves, Part 2

At almost every Catholic wedding that I have ever attended or officiated at, the first reading has been taken from Saint Paul's First Letter to the Corinthians, chapter 13. I'm sure you are all familiar with it. It is frequently called the "Hymn to Charity," and every line begins with "Love is."

Although by definition we monks do not marry, this chapter from First Corinthians is just as precious to us monks as it is to couples, and just as necessary—especially verses 7 and 8: "Love forgives all things, believes all things, hopes all things, endures all things. Love never comes to an end."

The greatest temptation that love faces is to "end"—to cease to exist, or to grow cold, or even to turn into its opposite—to become hatred. A monk friend of mine believes that this is impossible, that once the connection of love has formed between two people, it is indestructible. According to him, all love is eternal. Once it has been born it can never die. When I first heard him say this, thirty years ago, I thought it was beautiful. I still think it is beautiful; I only wonder if it is true. If it *is* true (say I)—if love is immortal—this can only be the case when it is divine love, when God's love has been accepted into a human heart and the human person lives out of that love—when he or she not only loves *as* God loves, but loves *with* God's love. In other words, when the Holy Spirit loves in and through me and when I in my liberty love with the power and the perseverance of the Holy Spirit.

From the earliest beginnings of Christian monasticism monks have tried to live this way, to love as God loves. Not only in the day-to-day ways described in the previous chapter, the ways of benevolence and disponibility that function smoothly when things are going well, but in adverse circumstances, in the heroic ways that are the only viable option: forgiveness, love of enemies, and vicarious suffering.

I hope that by this point in your reading you've discovered that what is absolutely central in the life of the monk is Jesus himself. The rest is commentary. It is in him that the monk finds grace and inspiration and example to keep going and keep seeking in his monastic vocation. And nowhere is the monk more Jesus' apprentice than in the art of difficult loving.

Jesus reveals himself as the teacher of forgiving love in response to a question from one of his disciples: "Master, how many times should I forgive my brother if he sins against me?" Peter, the disciple who poses the question, thinks that he himself may have the answer. He just wants to confirm it with Jesus. In a manner that seems to him reckless and extravagant—as do so many other aspects of the kingdom that Jesus preaches—Peter audaciously opens the possibility of going as far as seven times. How many times, Lord? Seven? As many as seven? Jesus teaches him and teaches every monk that the number seven doesn't even begin to express the number of times that pardon will be necessary in order to keep your brother as your brother. If you're only prepared for seven times, you might as well forget about the idea of having brothers, living in community with them, and taking in the full force of their imperfect personalities. Not even seven times seven is sufficient. Only an infinite number of times will be sufficient. Probably only after his death and resurrection did the disciples realize how many times Jesus had pardoned them, for offences that they had been too insensitive to recognize.

Monks have never doubted the correctness and necessity of Jesus' teaching on pardoning love, but often enough in concrete situations they have experienced the spontaneous reaction so perfectly expressed in the Portuguese word (always accompanied by an exclamation point) *Chega!* "I've had it!" At such moments, when the teaching of Jesus threatens to disappear from the life of a monastic community, the Spirit of Jesus inspires an individual monk to reaffirm the absolute and perennial importance of Jesus' words concerning pardon. Thus we have the Desert Fathers' story of a community that had decided to expel a monk for some repeated offence against one of its fundamental values. Suddenly they become aware that one of the holiest of the senior monks is packing his luggage and preparing to leave them. Profoundly distressed, they ask him where he is going. When he responds that he is merely obeying the communal decision that has just been made to cast out all incorrigible sinners—of whom he is the first (as Saint Paul said of himself)—the brethren recognize that it is they who have been unfaithful to Jesus' doctrine of forgiving love. "Love forgives all things." Chastened and converted, they come to a new conclusion: everyone gets to stay in the monastery.

At the very beginning of his proclamation of the kingdom, in the Sermon on the Mount, Jesus says something even more demanding about love: "Love your enemies." This teaching stretches from one end of the Gospel to the other—from the beginning of Jesus' preaching to his prayer on the cross for his executioners. He is not speaking only about the sentiment of love or only about works of love (such as, "If your enemy is thirsty, give him to drink") or only about freedom from resentment ("If you are angry, then be so without sin; the sun must not go down on your anger"). He is speaking about the whole complex reality of love: sentiment and action and inner reconciliation all at once. You *will* have enemies, Jesus assures his disciples. All will hate you for my sake. But in every possible way, you must continue to be peacemakers. No retaliation—none.

I hope you who are reading these pages can understand the struggle that this caused—and causes—for Christian monks. Jesus must have been aware of the shock he was creating by joining together in a single concept *love* and *enemy*, by insisting on holding together what naturally splits apart. Remember when he said in a certain case of diabolical possession that such demons could only be expelled by prayer and fasting? How many monks have spent years in prayer and fasting—with tears, as it says in the Letter to the Hebrews—in order to acquire that patient and tranquil heart that has overcome all temptation to enmity, to become Franciscan enough, to pray with all sincerity, "Where there is hatred, let me bring love"?

In his second volume of *Jesus of Nazareth*, Benedict XVI writes that for all the mysteriousness of the New Testament teaching of vicarious suffering—someone freely suffering in the place of another, taking on the sin of another—it is essential to its message. It is what Jesus did for us, as the Servant of Yahweh: "Surely he has borne our infirmities and carried our diseases." This love unto the end has also penetrated into the monastic tradition: "He loved me, and gave himself up for me." Perhaps here, in their great generosity, the nuns have an advantage over the monks. More than a few times, the medieval chronicles speak of nuns who have freely assumed the sufferings—physical, moral, or spiritual—of another. Someone has "reached the end of his strength," as the psalmist says, and another willingly supplies the strength of her prayer, her self-denial, and her inner combat to make up what is missing. What is it that Saint Paul writes: "I make up in my body what is lacking in the sufferings of Christ for the sake of his body, the Church" (Col 1:24)? My own suspicion is that many monasteries, and many other human communities, are kept going by the self-giving of unnamed persons for the sake of Christ's body the Church.

First Corinthians 13 is not about sentimental love, but about the possibilities of divine love in a human person, in a human community, possibilities first made visible and palpable in Jesus of Nazareth. If a young monk reads this chapter and his heart says, "That's what I want," it is a good sign. He has come to the right place.

Chapter Nineteen. *Salve Regina*

Truly, I ought to feel ashamed of myself. My patron, Saint Bernard, always used to say, *Numquam satis de Maria*—"It's impossible to say too much about Mary"—and looking back over the contents of this book thus far, I see that up to now I have said far too little. Let me try to make amends in this chapter and try to describe, at least in a rudimentary way, the important role that Our Lady plays in monastic spirituality.

Mary, for monks, is in the first place our sister, our older sister. It is she who in her manner of relating to God and to her fellow human beings has gone ahead of us and established the pattern of monastic spirituality. It would be natural to assume that Jesus is the model of the monastic life, and this is certainly true. But monastic life is essentially about being at the disposition of Jesus, being for Jesus, becoming united to Jesus, treating others as if they were Jesus. In all this Mary is the firstborn, the first to have had this kind of relationship with the Lord and the one who has left a permanent mark on this relationship. The biography of Mary as presented to us in the gospels—or, putting it another way, the events of Mary's life in the mysteries of the most holy rosary—is the synopsis of monastic life in story form.

Let us take the Joyful Mysteries as an example. In her response to God's messenger Gabriel at the Annunciation, Mary teaches us (as an older sister is obliged to teach her younger siblings) that life with God is *obedience*—the openness to a divine intelligence and a divine will that surpass our comprehension and at times summon us to carry out a task that far exceeds our possibilities, but that can become possible if our response is a believing *Fiat* (see the beautiful chapter 68 of the Rule of Saint Benedict, entitled "When the Monk is Asked to Carry out Impossible Tasks"). In her

Visitation to Saint Elizabeth, Mary instructs us in the *service and self-forgetfulness* that have to characterize anyone who calls himself or herself the "servant of the Lord." In the Nativity, Mary is *joyful adoration in circumstances of utter simplicity*: somehow the animals and the hay of the manger, instead of impoverishing Mary's contemplation of the Word made flesh, give it exactly the frame that is called for. Mary at the Presentation is the *humble fulfillment of the requirements of the Law* ("They had finished everything required by the law of the Lord," Luke 2:39)—the faithful accomplishment of what are traditionally called the "duties of our state of life," duties that all of us have, because every human being in his or her individuality lives in a definite state of life and pleases God precisely by carrying out the obligations of that state—be it husband or wife, priest or religious, teenager or senior citizen. And Mary in the loss and recuperation of Jesus in the Temple is *the acceptance of dedicating oneself to a Lord who constantly surprises us by his presence and by his absence*, his manifestations and his disappearances. As a matter of fact, every Christian who prays the rosary is a pupil in the school of Mary. What distinguishes the monk is that he really does everything possible to have the virtues of Mary become like "a seal upon his heart, a seal upon his arm" (Song 8.6).

Mary is not only the sister of us monks. She is also our mother. The early fathers of the church loved to call her the "new Eve," the real "mother of all the living." In monastic spirituality, together with the heavenly Father, Mary actively participates in generating the life of Christ within each one of us. In the physical order, the monastic writers say, Mary gave birth only once, to the child Jesus, in Bethlehem of Judah. But in the spiritual realm, Mary is the mother of Christ in the soul of every Christian. Since her Son Jesus is the head of a new humanity, since all of this transformed humanity is the mystical Body of her Son, in giving birth to Jesus Mary gives birth to all the members of Christ. She births Christ in every member of Christ. She transmits the life of Christ to everyone who accepts him. This is the mission that was given to her at the foot of the Cross: "Woman, behold your son" (John 19:26). This *behold* is of a tremendous intensity. It starts off, perhaps, signifying, "Look at your new son," and grows into meaning, "Accept the beloved disciple [symbol of each and all of us] as your new son," and ultimately becomes, "Show yourself to be the true mother of humankind, your new son," nourishing each one of the faithful with the milk of the Christ-life.

In one of the great Marian hymns, *Ave, maris stella*, the Church prays to Mary, *"Monstra te esse matrem"*—Show that you really are our mother. Treat us as a mother treats her children. Give us life. Give us, your sons and daughters, the immortal life of your divine Son. In the section of our Order's Constitutions that sets out the spirit of the Order, we read, "Each community of the Order and all the monks are dedicated to the Blessed Virgin Mary, Mother and Symbol of the Church in the order of faith, love and perfect union with Christ" (OCSO Const 3.4).

We have spoken of Mary as sister and as mother. She is also the Queen and the Lady of monks. In God's providence, our Cistercian monastic order began at the very end of the eleventh century and took root throughout Europe all through the twelfth century. This is the age of chivalry, the age of the troubadours, the age of the glorification of courtly love. All of this entered into the way the Cistercian monk understood—and continues to understand— his relationship with Mary. In a way that is perhaps difficult for post-modern men and women to understand, in a way that often requires years and years to become a reality among those who enter our monasteries in the twenty-first century, Mary for the monk is the beloved of his heart. It is not a romantic relationship in the contemporary understanding of the term; likewise, it is not a psychological compensation. Rather, through a genuine spiritual perception, slowly brought to birth, the monk perceives that within both the monastery and his own heart, there is a beloved feminine presence, blessing and pacifying and purifying the ambience of the cloister and the inner ambience of his soul.

This feminine presence is more personal, more specific than a Jungian archetype. It is the presence of a particular person; it is a very particular spiritual fragrance. It is Mary making herself known to the monk as companion, as friend, as Wisdom, as consolation—as communion in the midst of solitude. In the fifth joyful mystery, Mary learned by hard experience to accept Jesus as the one who comes and goes at will. Perhaps for this reason, and out of compassion for us, she has chosen to be ever present. Christ really does hide himself from us from time to time (and often enough for quite extended periods), just as the Father hid himself from him in the hours of Calvary. Mary is consistent in her own specific posture. As she chose to be present to Jesus even in the moment of his greatest dereliction, so she chooses to be present to us even in the moments when we suffer from divine abandonment. She is there at every moment—now and at the hour of our death.

A medieval tradition maintains that when Saint Bernard was preaching the Second Crusade in the cathedral of Speyer in Germany, as he came to the end of the already existent prayer of the *Salve Regina,* he was lifted out of himself and spontaneously added three acclamations that since then comprise its conclusion: "O clement, O loving, O sweet Virgin Mary." Bernard truly understood the love that unites Mary and the monk. Not for nothing is he called the *doctor marianus.*

Part II

The Making of a Monk

Chapter Twenty. The Monastic Vocation: An Exchange of Experiences

What kind of person becomes a monk? What are the motivations that lead young people to think seriously about the monastic life? Are they running away from something? Could a normal person become a monk? How do their families react? What does the process of becoming a monk consist of? What are the ups and downs that a young monk encounters in the initial years—the so-called years of formation? Why do some people persevere and others leave? Is the monastic life a happy life? An easy life? A tough life?

It might seem pretentious for me to imagine that people in general are interested in the answers to these questions. But as a matter of fact, I'm not imagining. Monastic life, and monks and nuns in particular, do stimulate a good amount of curiosity, judging by such factors as the requests we get for newspaper interviews, groups of visitors that come to pass a day in the monastery, the success of recent films such as *The Great Silence* (about Carthusian monks) and *Of Gods and Men* (about Trappist monks), and the flow of letters, phone calls, and emails that makes its way into the monastery. What is behind this interest? Personally, I would say that it's something deeper than mere curiosity. I believe that there's a degree of truth in the affirmation of the existence of a monastic archetype—that is to say, of the existence of a universal monastic dimension in each and every human person. Obviously, in the great majority of cases, this is not the archetype that will come to predominate when it comes to making a choice of career or lifestyle. Nonetheless, there is a bit of the monk in each person, and every once in a while that bit begins to glow when it comes in contact with a book or article about monastic life, or when an image of a monk or nun in habit appears on the television or computer screen.

Saint Paul says that we have received "different gifts" according to the disposition of the Holy Spirit. Fine. Who am I to disagree with Saint Paul? But I think it would be possible to say (and actually, he would be the first one to do so) that these different gifts are interlocking gifts and overlapping gifts, rather than gifts in complete isolation from each other. Each one of us has received a stocking full of gifts, and each one of us decides, in our human liberty—guided by God's inspiration, but in liberty all the same—what will be the particular gift that we will most develop. The wonderful thing is that the other gifts do not wither away or disappear; they remain as potentialities to be developed and integrated into the healthy development of the particular gift.

An obvious example would be marriage and consecrated celibacy. God has made us in such a way that the desire for affective and sexual fulfillment and stable union with another person is a reality for absolutely everybody. What happens to that desire if people accept what they believe is a call to consecrated chastity? Do they then place that desire under their pillows trusting that the next morning it will be gone, carried off by the angels? Certainly not! They have in front of them a long, sometimes arduous, and ultimately joyful task of weaving this desire into his call to consecrated chastity. They have the task of learning to live friendship, love, and community in a way that completes and enhances their celibate commitment. Frequently I tell young monks who are still discerning in their first years whether their call is to monastic life or married life, "It's both. But you have to find out in your particular case what's the tree and what's the vine. Is marriage the central trunk of your life around which a love of prayer and solitude and simplicity can beautifully entwine itself, or is religious life the solid trunk—is personal fulfillment in God and gift of self to God the tree—around which the desire for human companionship and shared interests and long, profound conversations will grow and flower? What's the tree and what's the vine?"

I'm assuming that for a good number of my readers marriage is the tree and the monastic archetype is the vine. Obviously, my situation is the opposite. For me, personal union with God in Christ is the tree—the tree whose trunk gets taller and wider every year, as new rings are added to it—and friendship and intimacy with others is the vine that learns to grow around the tree. Let's make a deal, then. Let's agree to complete one another. I'll share with you something of what it's like to have the monastic archetype as the predominant facet of my personality, and you share with me what it's like to have a different one at the center of your personality. How are we going to do this?

Here we meet with an initial paradox, namely, that I as a silent Trappist monk have access to all of you through the medium of the printed page, whereas you, who theoretically have no restrictions on your communication, don't have a way to get directly in touch with me. Shall we do it by telepathy, then? Prayer would be a better way than telepathy, or you could send an email to the publisher that would eventually find its way to me, or you could send a note to the monastery. Actually, telepathy is not as strange as it seems. That is to say, if you read these pages and something touches you and you reflect on them, somehow, mysteriously, I am not left untouched by your experience. Obviously, I am not specifically conscious of your individual experience—I do not suddenly feel a mystical breeze on my face—but I am enriched by the fact that my words have spoken to you, in an indescribable but very real way. All communication is a two-way street: if my words touch you then your being touched affects me.

By the way, there's some evidence that the monastic archetype is gaining new adherents. Especially in Europe, the percentage of people who live in a one-person household is very much on the rise. At times this is interpreted in a negative manner: the one-person household is seen as composed of people living against their will in an imposed solitude, or as the result of abandonment or a failed relationship. Of course, there must be a certain number of cases like that. At the same time, I know from personal contacts, in Europe, in the United States, and here in Brazil, that there are many freely chosen one-person households. There are many people whom God calls to be monastics in the broad sense, living this vocation/this personal decision outside the walls of a classical monastery. Often these are men and women of assiduous prayer, of great generosity, with substantial creative gifts and often with a part-time engagement in volunteer social work. Sometimes they group themselves into loose associations; sometimes they prefer to remain simply as individuals.

I think of a Cuban painter whom I got to know in my early twenties, shortly after my conversion to Catholicism, a painter who lived alone in a loft in Manhattan, in voluntary poverty, chastity, and obedience to his spiritual director. For several years, I visited him once a month, and he would speak to me about the spiritual life. I was twenty or twenty-one when he asked me, "Do you know that the Virgin Mary is the most beautiful creature that God ever created?" As a new Catholic, I really *didn't* know; it took me many years to come to see what he could so clearly see in his illuminated heart. He, without a doubt, was a person whom the monastic archetype (together with the artistic archetype) over-whelmingly molded and formed. Some of you reading this reflection are probably in the same situation.

Let all of this serve as an introduction to the second part of this book, on the making of a monk. In the following chapter, I hope to begin to answer, at least indirectly, the question I posed: What kind of person becomes a monk? Pray for those who do so. By our vocation as monks we are committed to pray for you. And you, by your vocation as fellow human beings, as our brothers and sisters, are committed to pray for us.

Chapter Twenty-One. The Birth of a Monastic Vocation

Just a few years ago, Pope Francis beatified a twentieth-century French Carmelite, Henri Gialou (Père Marie-Eugène), author of a well-known study on the spirituality of his order. The title of the first volume is a quotation from Saint Teresa of Avila: "I want to see God." Those words express in a remarkably clear and complete way what attracts a man or woman to the monastic life.

According to the Catholic contemplative tradition, desire is only possible as the consequence of experience. We can only desire what we have already tasted in some way. And this is exactly how a monastic vocation starts. One day a child (often it begins as early as that), a teenager, or a young adult senses in the midst of ordinary activities that behind and beneath all things and all acts there is a mystery that continually upholds, enlivens, and renews all that exists. There is a fountain out of which everything arises, a fountain of life that irrigates all life. The surface of the world peels back, and the young person glimpses the center, the burning core—burning, but not destroying, like the burning bush.

This mystery, although it is indefinable, has characteristics proper to it. It is holy: in its presence, in the moment of experience, you feel compelled to make some gesture—to bow down, to take off your shoes, to close your eyes, to sing. It is personal. You may not know its name, but you know that it has a name, and that in fact it is not something but someone. More than that: it is someone, *par excellence*. It is beautiful, and good, and true. And above all, it is love. It is the love at the origin of the universe, and it invites you into communion with itself, a communion that has in fact existed ever since you existed (if not before), and that now awaits your word of commitment.

Is there something that disposes a young person to such an experience? To begin with, it is crucial to affirm that what is taking place is a genuine interpersonal experience and not simply an encounter with one's own subjectivity. For the person who has such an experience, it is an authentic meeting with another, another more real than any other person could possibly be. That is the great conviction that remains after such an experience. I have seen the Real; I have touched the Real. He showed himself to me. Of this I am sure.

That said, I think there is a kind of person more inclined to such an encounter—more prepared for it, we might say. It is someone who from a very young age has lived within himself, lived in his own company. Living exposed to the beauty of nature can orient a person in this direction. Being a passionate reader can also do it. Suffering can also dispose a person in this way. A contentment with and even a preference for solitude is another way of being inwardly readied for the moment of revelation. If you read the first few paragraphs of Athanasius's *Life of Anthony*, you will find most of these qualities included in the description of Anthony's childhood. A comfortableness with, an attraction to, one's own inner world prepares a person to meet what is more inward to himself than he himself is. That is how Saint Augustine puts it in speaking about God in his *Confessions: interior intimo meo*. "You are more interior to me than my most interior self."

Even if this experience of God takes place very early in life, it would not be wrong to describe it as contemplation. It is not contemplation as the fruit of years of ascetical labor and moral dedication. It is pure gift. It is God introducing himself, presenting himself, and saying, "Stay with me." Remember how the disciples on the road to Emmaus said to the risen but as yet unrecognized Christ, *Mane nobiscum*, "Stay with us"? That is what a boy or girl, a teenager or young adult hears God saying to him or her: "Stay with me."

Certainly that is what the person himself wants. The same Teresa of Avila whom we quoted at the beginning of this chapter writes in her *Interior Castle* that once we have had this kind of gracious, genuine, unexpected contact with God, the only thing we want is to keep on having it. She describes the experience as drinking something so delicious and so satisfying that after having tasted it, no other drink can quiet our thirst. We think of Jesus promising the Samaritan woman "living water" (John 4:10). Teresa herself was probably inspired by this gospel incident when she came to speak about a person's first true contemplative experience.

When Jesus says in John's gospel that whoever drinks the water that he gives will never thirst again, he does not mean that the person will cease to have spiritual thirst. Rather, he means that such a person will never thirst for anything else, that all his thirst will be a thirst for God. Understanding this clearly, however—understanding that the one thing I want is to see God and abide with him—is usually the result not of a single experience, but of repeated experiences, scattered through one's childhood and adolescence. In the first place, many people who are granted the grace of such experiences don't know in the beginning that these are experiences of God. They are experiences of the Absolute, perhaps, or experiences of Being. Especially for young people brought up in non-religious households it can take a long time, a lot of research (of diverse kinds), and a lot of reflection before they are able to understand that the "name" of this personal holy One giving himself to be experienced is "God."

Then there is the more practical question. Are there really places in the world where I can dedicate myself wholeheartedly to this desire? Are there other people who do this? Who do it together? I know (a young person might well say to himself) that there are law schools and medical schools and diplomatic schools, but is there such a thing as a God school? People called to the monastic life intuit—if they know about them—that they will not find what they are looking for in a diocesan seminary or in an apostolic religious community. Where then, as the great hymn in Job 28 puts it, is the dwelling-place of Wisdom? I can testify to this truth from my own experience. At nineteen, I was consumed with the need to get away, to find a place where I could think and pray, be with God and find God. On my own I wasn't able to identify such a place. Thanks be to God, I asked some Catholic friends of mine at the university. For them the answer was im-mediate and obvious: "Go to a monastery." Even then, it took a bit of convincing on their part to persuade me that monasteries still existed and that they hadn't all been dissolved at the time of the Protestant Reformation. (You have to remember that I was a Jewish boy growing up in a Protestant country.)

This is truly the profile of the young men who come knocking at our door (as we used to say in the pre-Internet days). They are people who have glimpsed God and fallen in love with what they have seen. In their own humble way, they have had an experience like that of Abraham, Moses, and Isaiah. God has revealed himself to them. They are full of doubts and fears, both about the monastic community and about themselves (Are you crazy? Am I crazy?). But deeper than all these doubts and fears is the desire to "live in the house of the Lord forever," to integrate themselves into a community that has no other purpose than to seek and find his face. It is moving and humbling to hear them tell what God has said to their hearts and what their hearts have said to God.

Chapter Twenty-Two.
For This Was I Born

In the monastery in Massachusetts where I first entered the Trappist Order, the monks make their living by making jelly (as we do here by making cookies). New members of the community are usually put to work taking the filled jelly jars off the belt, putting them into boxes, sealing the boxes with special tape, and stacking the boxes onto pallets to be taken off for shipping. It's a rapid-movement process, and it shouldn't leave any time for idle conversation—but it does, at least for those who haven't yet experienced an inner attraction to silence.

One morning, in the midst of work in the jelly factory, the young brother who was next to me on the assembly line asked, "When did you first know that this was it for you?" Translation: "When did you first really know that you were called to be a monk in this monastery?" It was a question that required absolutely no time for reflection. The memory was as clear as a bell, because the moment was the moment of the ringing of the bells for the Divine Office. I had arrived at the monastery for my first visit five minutes before the ringing of the bells for Vespers, and when the three bells pealed out their solemn and joyful sound (each bell with its own name: the little soprano bell, Mary, the medium baritone bell, Bernard, and the great bass bell, Joseph), my heart said, "This is it. This is the place." The other monk stopped and stared at me in astonishment, causing a momentary traffic jam in the packing process. "What is it?" I asked, seeing his expression. "But that's exactly *my* experience," he answered. "It was when I heard the abbey bells ring for the first time that I knew that this was the place where I was going to spend the rest of my life."

That co-incidence (in the most literal sense of the word) might be due in part to the fact that both of us are musicians—for years I was cantor in the monastery and he the principal organist—so bells get to us. On the other hand, there is always a moment like this for everyone destined to be a monk, a moment that is described in poetic language as the shock of recognition and in more ordinary speech as Wow!

This is the centuries-old and always new experience of the candidate for the monastic life. It is the experience that Jesus describes in two parables dear to the monastic heart, both from Matthew 13: the comparison of the kingdom of God to a treasure buried in a field, and the comparison of the kingdom of God to a pearl of great price, to obtain which a man sells everything he has. Anybody can visit a monastery and be delighted with the liturgy, the friendliness of the monks, the beauty of the buildings, the charm of the silence, and a million other things, but the person called to be a monk has a radically different experience. And it always comes down to this: "This is the kingdom of God, the holy city, the new Jerusalem." Unlike other career choices, unlike other processes of reflection with regard to a possible priestly or religious vocation, the person called to be a monk does not make a discernment. He does not make a list of pros and cons; he does not judiciously ponder the appropriateness of a monastic vocation for someone with his personality profile. No; he is knocked off his feet. He is the object of a revelation: God tells him, by something that surges up within his heart, "You have arrived. You have reached the end of your pilgrimage. From now on, your pilgrimage will take place in this simple spot. You can put your knapsack down."

I think you can imagine the joy that a young man or woman feels at having found his place in the world, at having had the immense fortune of being allotted the best place of all. The candidate for the monastery feels exactly what the psalmist expresses in Psalm 16: "The lot marked out for me is my delight: welcome indeed the heritage that falls to me."

This exultation of spirit applies not only to the vocation as such, but to the brothers who make up the monastic community, the buildings that form the architectural complex, the particular way of doing things—sacred things and day-to-day things—that a specific monastic community has developed over the course of generations. Even the smell of the monastery is unique and blessed. I remember on my initial visits to Spencer (my first monastery) that I knew that I was home again when a very definite smell, which I have never experienced in any other place, filled my nostrils and produced in me a profound sigh of peace and contentment. For another candidate, the quiet glory of the monastery revealed itself in the singing of the trees. "I can hear the trees singing," he would say to me, his eyes shining. "Can you?"

All of this is the work of the Holy Spirit. The Constitutions of our Order say that "The Providence of God calls a person to *this* place and to *this* group of brothers." God means to sanctify a young man and prepare him for eternal life in the kingdom of heaven by making him enter and persevere for his entire life in this particular monastery. In order to win him to the vocation that will be his salvation, God has to dazzle the candidate. So he opens the young man's eyes to the glory that fills the monastery and its monks, glory that is genuine and ever-present but that is usually concealed behind the "cloud of unknowing." God is like Solomon showing all of the treasures of his palace to the queen of Sheba. And the candidate experiences the same joyful dizziness as her Royal Highness did when she came from the ends of the earth to meet with Solomon: "When the queen of Sheba had observed all the wisdom of Solomon, the house that he had built, the food of his table, the seating of his officials and the attendance of his servants, their clothing, his valets and his burnt offerings that he offered in the house of the Lord, there was no more spirit in her" (1 Kgs 10:4-5). The Bible has found exactly the right word to define the state of spirit of the candidate: All the wind—spirit—has been knocked out of him. He is breathless.

Has the candidate been placed under a spell? Has someone brainwashed him? You will remember from the foregoing chapter that I said that a person with a contemplative vocation probably will have had in his childhood or adolescent years an experience of the sacred mystery that underlies and upholds creation. That mystery infinitely transcends space and time, and yet it touches specific times and places and makes them holy, and it touches specific people at specific moments and makes them capable of perceiving the flood of holiness that inundates such a place.

Remember what Jacob said when he awoke from his dream of seeing the angels of God ascending and descending: " 'Surely the Lord is in this place—and I did not know it!' And he was afraid, and said, 'How awesome is this place! This is none other than the house of God, and this is the gate of heaven' " (Gen 28:16-17). For the Jewish people, the holy of holies was the Temple. And the candidate, from the very first visit, feels—knows—that he has come to his temple, to the temple of the Lord and his own, to his Mecca. That is why he loves psalms such as 26, 27, 84: "O Lord, I love the house where you dwell, the place where your glory abides"; "There is one thing I ask of the Lord—to live in the house of the Lord all the days of my life"; "How lovely is your dwelling place, Lord, God of hosts." Yes, that is one of the surest signs of a monastic vocation—this desire and this amazingly rapidly formed and yet totally valid conviction: "In the Lord's own house will I dwell forever and ever."

A thank you to my readers for allowing me to experience anew the overwhelming joy of my first contact with the monastery.

Chapter Twenty-Three. Observership

If the fire that flared up in the candidate on visiting the monastery was not merely a *fogo de palha*—a straw fire that burns itself out in a matter of moments—but a "fire in the bones," as the Scriptures say, the candidate will keep coming back to the guesthouse on retreats and will eventually be invited to spend a few months inside the enclosure, living within the community.

This transition is always a shock. However much the young man believed he was already experiencing monastic life during his time in the guesthouse, he now discovers that life within the enclosure is something quite different. The difference is a question of intensity. Everything is more intense: the climate of silence, the encounter with solitude, the relentlessness of the monastic day surprisingly full of activities: the hours of the Divine Office, the times for *lectio divina* and private prayer, the periods of manual labor, the daily classes for those in formation, the constant togetherness with the community in the liturgy, at work, and at meals, the weekly meeting with the spiritual director. (We sometimes allow a religious from another congregation to pass several months within the enclosure in order to "re-invigorate" his own vocation. Recently we had a young priest who figured out that there are thirty-six monastic activities every day and ticked them off in his notebook one by one on a daily basis.)

And just as there is an intensity of the encounter with so much that is new and unexpected, so there is an intensity of absence: the disappearance of almost everything well-known and familiar. Friends and family are far away and out of reach, as are shopping malls and movie theaters. There is no weekend in the monastery. Instead there is the new reality called Sunday: a day without manual work, to be sure, but not exactly a day off, a day to relax.

It is a day of more solemnity in the liturgy, with special moments of prayer such as Benediction of the Blessed Sacrament or a communal rosary, and a day of sacred leisure, with time for reading, solitary walks in the woods, or perhaps the cultivation of a simple hobby. Whatever the day of the week, snacking does not exist. You eat at mealtimes, and that's it. Sports are replaced by physical labor. It is another world.

That is the truth of the matter. The observer finds himself in a completely different culture. Amazing! Just a few miles away—at arm's reach—is the old cherished culture in which everyone he has ever known up to now lives and breathes, and here within the enclosure is another culture, the monastic culture. What makes the experience even more intense is that in the monastery people enter the community one by one, not in classes, as in the Jesuits or the Franciscans. And so the young observer finds himself in a new culture, totally strange for him but totally familiar for everybody else (or so he thinks). Everybody else knows when to bow and kneel in church; everybody else knows the basics of sign language (which still exists to some extent in Trappist monasteries). He is the only "foreigner."

And yet, for all this difference and intensity, the hallmark of the time of observership is joy. At the time of solemn vows (seven to ten years after the moment the observer is presently living), he will pray in the abbey church, "Receive me, Lord, as you have promised and I will live; do not disappoint me in my hope." The observer does not need to pray in this way as yet. He is anything but disappointed. For him the new culture he has entered into is a land of marvels.

What are the things that especially strike observers who come to our monasteries? Without a doubt, the elders. Young observers are fascinated by the elder members of the community. They are astonished at the fidelity of community members of eighty or ninety years of age, who take active part in all of the activities of the monastic day. The observers are deeply moved by the elders' humility and their tendency to take the last place, to make themselves invisible, even though they have every right to be treated as honored seniors. The newcomers are touched by their unvarying goodness, by their virtue, which is 100% natural, with no

artificial ingredients added. They are overwhelmed by the friendship that the elders offer them with no strings attached and that
is expressed with great dignity and delicacy: a smile, a word of
encouragement, a brief note at their place in the refectory. The
newcomers glimpse their future in the elderly, and suddenly old
age is no longer a time to be feared, a time of diminishment and
decrepitude, but rather a wonderful autumn, an autumn like the
kind they have in Japan or New England, where just before the
leaves fall from the trees, they are transformed into a splendor of
reds and yellows and golds. The young observer comes to experience personally the concrete truth of the "beautiful elder," a monk
or nun made beautiful from the inside, with a gentle light that
illuminates every object upon which it falls.

But it's not just the elders that impress observers. They are
taken aback by the warmth and the affection of the whole community. An observer is genuinely surprised to learn that there is
no period of probation to go through before he can be considered
one of the brothers. From the very first day, he feels himself treated
as a member of the community. People go out of their way to
explain things to him; brothers help him to perform the tasks that
in time will become simple but initially appear impossible. The
brothers show interest in how he is adapting, or whether there is
anything he needs. They find a way to let him know that they are
praying for him, that they hope that he is happy, that they are
there for him, that if it is God's will they would be pleased for
him to persevere in the community.

In a healthy monastery (and, thank God, there are many of
them), there truly is a family atmosphere. The monks are all doing
their best to live out the great chapter on fraternal relations from
the Rule of Saint Benedict, chapter 72: "They should each try to
be the first to show respect to the other, supporting with the greatest patience one another's weaknesses of body or behavior, and
earnestly competing in obedience to one another. No one is to
pursue what he judges better for himself, but instead, what he
judges better for someone else. To their fellow monks they show
the pure love of brothers."

I have spoken of the people who make a strong impression on
those just starting out in monastic life. But the monastery, as Saint

Bernard describes it in his commentary on the Song of Songs, is first and foremost the "house of God," and the great fact of the observership is the new way of interacting with the master of the house. All kinds of unscheduled encounters with God occur. Turning a corner in the cloister, looking out the library window, listening to a professed monk give a class on monastic observances—and suddenly, God shows up unannounced. Not as someone perceptible to the senses, and not as an idea or a feeling, either. All the same, it is he: undeniably he. Saint Bernard calls these unscheduled encounters "visits of the Word." In these visits, Bernard writes, God draws near in such a way that you are only aware of his approach when he is already present. His arrival always catches you by surprise, and his departure has already occurred before you knew that he was leaving.

When observers ponder what is taking place, they recognize that the spiritual beauty of the elder monks and the availability and generosity of the younger ones are also visits of the Word, a Word that has inhabited the bodies and souls of the brother monks for many years and assimilated them to itself. The special cleanliness and brightness of things in the monastery—a mug, a table, a pair of polished shoes—are likewise not accidents. So it really is true, after all, observers say to themselves: "The Spirit of the Lord fills the world." And they are not just quoting the Scriptures but touching the source from which the Scriptures flow. Observers come to the conclusion that it would be the blessing of blessings to live continually exposed to this benign influence, which ripens and sanctifies and illuminates and unites us to itself. As yet they are still unaware of the price of this blessing (even blessings have prices; perhaps especially blessings), but an inner decision is slowly maturing: to remain in the light, to stay within the circle of Christ's light, here in the monastery, where it shines in such a special way, and to let the light do its work, whatever that implies. That decision, that "whatever," will lead the observer to ask the abbot to admit him into the community and permit him to take the next steps in monastic formation.

Chapter Twenty-Four. *Fervor Novitius*

With so much holiness all around him—in the liturgy, the buildings, the brothers, and everything that belongs to the house of God—the novice (who has now completed his observership, gone home to spend a last few weeks with family and friends, and returned to join the community for good) says to himself, "Why not me?" Everything in the monastery is holy, and I will be holy too. Probably the new novice, in his heart of hearts (where he himself does not yet see things as they are), imagines that for the most part, he already is holy. One of my most embarrassing recollections—embarrassing and humorous—is how I, at the end of my observership, knelt at my bedside, looked at the crucifix above my bed, and said in all sincerity to God, "Well, Lord, you've done an awful lot in cleaning up my life over these past few months. It's true that there was much that needed correction, but you have succeeded in purifying me of almost everything. If by any chance there still remains any inner work to be done when I return to the novitiate, I want you to know that you have my full permission to go ahead and cleanse me of these last remaining cobwebs." If I had only known that God hadn't even gotten started at this point! If I could only have heard his compassionate, loving laughter at my presumption!

But in fact observers never do see and never do hear. Probably if they saw and heard, if they had the least idea of all the years that lay between them and holiness (*if* by the mercy of God they are destined to someday attain holiness—which is a big "if," and with a holiness very different from the kind they initially imagined), they would never return to the monastery after the observership. "Nice experience," they would say, "but not for me."

The atmosphere of holiness that observers sense all about them make the freshly minted novice say, *Santo subito* (Sainthood now!) in regard to his own monastic project. Now *Santo subito* might work when it comes to the official canonization of a recently deceased person of indubitable holiness who has spent the whole of a long and arduous lifetime in absolute dedication to the fulfillment of God's will, as in the famous case of Pope John Paul II. However, it is not a realistic program for spiritual growth during this present life. The only people whom God (God, I say, and not we ourselves) is going to sanctify in record time are people that he plans to call to his kingdom at a very young age—Thérèse of Lisieux, Dominic Savio, Maria Goretti. God's sanctification of us always takes an entire lifetime—we can go as far as to say that the length of one's life coincides with the amount of time God has determined as necessary for getting us ready for the kingdom of heaven—and if we are going to live for many years on this earth, God's transforming work is going to need all these years to get us to the omega point he has established. A monk destined to live until eighty is not going to be holy at twenty. At the most, there will be a few tender buds on his branches to give a humble hope of future sanctity.

But it is exactly this that the new monk doesn't understand, and perhaps simply can't understand. According to Cassian in book twelve of his *Institutes*, the first of the passions to take hold of a human being (and thus closely associated with original sin) and the last to let go of us is the idea that the universe exists for my personal realization and that I myself will bring the process to completion. It doesn't much matter what the particular project of self-fulfillment is. Every one of us believes that the world exists in order for me to get to the top of the ladder, and that I am perfectly capable of scaling it without help from anybody else. It is an illusion, of course. But it is universal. Young monks succumb to it too.

To a certain extent this is the explanation of the phenomenon called *fervor novitius*—first fervor, or novice's fervor. It is a tremendous surge of energy that emerges from the conviction that holiness is just a sprint away; I only have to move as fast and as hard as I can to grasp the prize and make it mine.

The novice in pursuit of instant holiness creates a program of rapid-fire sanctification. By the way, he normally sets about doing so without informing his novice master. Some instinct warns him that the novice master will be all for moderation and one step at a time, whereas the novice knows that that will never get him anywhere. Much better, certainly, than "one step at a time" is a confidently administered command: "Full speed ahead."

This program has certain cardinal points, to which the novice of this type is punctiliously faithful. We could even call them commandments. What are they? Let me describe two interrelated ones that will, I hope, give you some idea of the whole package.

1. More is better. The monastic life in itself is always exacting and rigorous. There are vigils, fasting, personal prayer, poverty, silence, and many other practices. The fervent novice perceives that in the monastery all of these are practiced faithfully by the brothers but still, not as much as is humanly possible. The novice is tempted (and often enough gives in to his temptation) to crank up the level of his ascetical engagement: to eat less, sleep less, talk less, own less. (Perhaps I should have said "Less is better" rather than "more," but I was referring to the degree of ascetical engagement.) Sometimes this can lead to a novice trying to live with a minimum of furniture in his cell, a minimum of verbal exchange with his fellow monks, a minimum of food, drink, and sleep.

One hopes that the novice master or mistress is keeping a close watch over their novices (as the Rule of Saint Benedict prudently mandates), because occasionally these exaggerations can lead to physical or psychological problems. There is a certain degree of generosity involved in what such novices are undertaking, but there is also a lot of narcissism mixed up with it. This narcissism remains invisible to novices, because, as they understand it, narcissism has to do with self-indulgence, and what they are trying to do is the very opposite of self-indulgence.

God willing, if the novice perseveres and matures, he will come to grasp the wisdom of Cassian's affirmation: "Extremes meet." One extreme is the mirror image of its opposite. The self-indulgence of gluttony is at its root identical to the self-indulgence of excessive fasting. An inability to greet one's fellow monk stems from the same difficulty as the compulsive need to make contact. For the extreme faster and extreme feaster, food is an equally problematic issue. Both the absolutely mute monk and his exaggeratedly verbal companion (it is not rare to encounter such pairs in the same novitiate) are still profoundly unskilled in the art of human communication.

2. Holiness is found in the externals. The young novice, newly hatched, cannot as yet intuit much of spiritual reality. What Origen calls the "spiritual senses" (in *Contra Celsum*)— interior sensibilities analogous to the five physical senses— which enable us to perceive and respond to God's inward and delicate interventions, have not yet been activated in him. For this reason, for the novice the sensibly palpable is the real. It is much easier for him to identify and respond to an ascetical project of his own devising than to the gentle inspirations of grace. That is why an intense fast or a prayer marathon is much more attractive to him than the simple act of renouncing his self-will when obedience demands it, or the basic generosity involved in participating in all the activities of the monastic day, both the agreeable ones and the disagreeable ones.

God uses the first fervor of novices as a means of rooting them in the monastic life. (God is the most ecological of all beings: he never wastes *anything*.) He is willing to accept the self-love and the self-centeredness of novices for the time being, in order to let them make some initial progress, and because the novices are too blind to be capable of anything else at the present. God accepts the limited good he finds in the present and is already planning greater and deeper things for the future. He has his dream for each novice. Little by little he will transform that dream into a fact. That is how he deals with each of us, and not just novices.

Chapter Twenty-Five.
The First Major Crisis

One morning, one of the most idealistic monks in our community came to me with an unusual request. "I want to have a crisis." "Why would you want to have a crisis?" I asked him. "Because everyone else in the novitiate says that they're going through one, and I think I'm missing an opportunity for growth." I promised him that in God's good time he would certainly have a crisis—more than one, probably, but until Divine Providence saw fit to send him a crisis he should just sit back and enjoy the ride. As a matter of fact, God did get around to sending him a crisis, and when it finally came, it came full strength. Fortunately, he was able to pass through it and persevere in his vocation.

Probably most of us have heard that in Chinese, the ideogram for *crisis* is composed of two images: the image for *risk* and the image for *opportunity*. A crisis is a risk that could turn out to be a marvelous opportunity. Could turn out to be—but it's not inevitable that it will turn out to be. That's why it's a risk.

The most common crises in the novitiate stem from one of three factors, or a combination of all three: the self you left behind at the monastery gate, the self you brought in through the monastery gate, and the self that your brothers brought in with them. This kind of crisis is probably universal in any serious endeavor that aims at permanent commitment. I will give you the monastic version of the story.

You have not forgotten the monastic beginner of the last chapter, overflowing with zeal, even if not a "zeal according to knowledge," as Saint Paul puts it (Rom 10:2). During the time of his initial fervor, everything in the monastery seemed wonderful to

him, and the new monk believed that he had completely identified himself with the monastic project. In fact, however, one of
the things that cause a monastic crisis to hit is the discovery that
very little of the person has actually entered the monastic life. I'm
not talking about laziness or lack of generosity. After a certain
amount of time, every monk, even the most generous and well
balanced, comes to experience that his whole world of references,
relationships, enjoyments, and interests is back home—not in the
monastery in Campo do Tenente but in the interior of Minas or
the beaches of Rio or the center of Brasília. Theoretically, the novice was aware of all that he was leaving behind when he entered.
The abbot and the novice master, obliged in conscience, tried to
emphasize to the candidate this whole sacrificial dimension of
the monastic life and to question him repeatedly as to his real
willingness to give up so much.

But as Saint John of the Cross says, states of soul are like the
weather. They are all-encompassing (see *Dark Night of the Soul,*
2.7.5). Just as on a warm and sunny day it's almost impossible to
remember the bone-piercing chill of a day of torrential rains and
an overcast sky, so for the candidate, filled with the desire to give
himself to God in the monastic life, it is impossible to experience
what it's like to be deprived of everything that formerly made up
his world. And to be deprived of one's world in such a way is
tantamount to being deprived of one's very self. In some way, we
are the nexus of relationships, associations, habits, objects, and
places in which we are inserted. So when this crisis comes—this
crisis of unbelievably intense nostalgia (Portuguese has a marvelous untranslatable word for this: *saudades*)—the novice may feel
that he is undergoing the loss of his deepest being. Perhaps he
recalls at this juncture the words of Jesus, "Whoever loves his
own life more than me is not worthy of me" (see Matt 10:37 and
Luke 14:26). Should he remember them, they will be hard words
to him, iron words that shackle, and not divine words that transform and liberate.

What will the novice do? Will he do his best to persevere, giving himself and life in the monastery the time necessary for a
gradual re-construction of himself within the enclosure, a gradual
formation of a new world of references within the monastic com-

munity? Or will he find the pull to the self that he left behind irresistible? It's impossible to predict the outcome. Just about every novice goes through this crisis of finding himself in exile within the monastery. Some cling with all their might and redis-cover themselves in the monastery; others can validly discover that they were mistaken in their initial enthusiasm and that their real self is awaiting them back in the place they came from. The important thing is that the decision not be made on the basis of inward emotional pressures, however strong they may be. When a novice enters into this kind of crisis, I tell him that the most important thing is to wait to find out what God wants for him, because in that divine will the source of the person's lasting hap-piness will be found: Wait for a revelation. I am convinced that the person who holds out through the storm of his feelings will come to hear the still, small voice of God orienting him to his true future.

So much for the self left behind at the monastery gate, and the decision that has to be taken about whether to bring him slowly into the cloister or follow him back outside. The second factor that can set a crisis in motion is precisely the encounter with the self that the young monk brought in. We've already made refer-ence to the great degree of self-idealization that characterizes the first steps of a monastic vocation. For a person who suffers from the low self-esteem so characteristic of contemporary culture, finding oneself in the order, cleanliness, and silence of the mon-astery normally produces a strong sensation of relief, well-being, and self-acceptance. All the unacceptable aspects of the self seem to have miraculously vaporized. They don't exist anymore. And in fact there is usually an initial space of time in the monastery (generally a number of months) when the person experiences himself as pacified and unified. All those impulses to irritation, all that complicated sexual energy, all the envy experienced when looking at others, all the sad self-rejection, all the driving ambition and the need to accumulate objects—it all seems solved. This calm is a mysterious reality. It is not the result of a tremendous applica-tion of willpower and self-control; nor is it an exercise in self-delusion. Simply, the initial experience of living in the monastery generates a profound peace. The only thing that the new monk desires is that it go on forever. Actually, he doesn't even desire this, because he assumes that it will go on forever—this marvelous *pax benedictina*.

I believe (on the basis of the writings of our twelfth-century fathers) that in some way these months of "peace like a river," as the prophet Isaiah puts it (Isa 66:12), are a genuine foretaste of what monastic life will really be at the end of the journey. They are an infused anticipatory grace that God pours into our heart to strengthen us in the struggles that are to come, and that do not delay in their arrival. For suddenly, from one day to the next, the scenario changes and the novice gets back, with interest, his whole disordered psycho-spiritual existence. It didn't go away after all. On the contrary, after these months of remission, it erupts anew with unexpected violence.

A question imposes itself with tremendous insistence: Now that I have learned that this fragmented, conflicted me whom I thought myself free of continues to be me—that I am he, that he is my inseparable companion or, better, myself as I truly am and that entrance into the monastic life has not delivered me from "me"—do I choose to remain here for the long haul and expose him to the slow and at times painful healing to be applied by Jesus and the monastic community, or do I give up? It is possible to decide to desist. No, the monk can say to himself. It was bad enough facing up to my unpleasant side in the relative comfort of the outside world, where it's possible to hide it a good portion of the time. It's asking too much that I face it twenty-four hours a day, full force, and with all the "hard and arduous elements" of the monastic life, as the Rule puts it. It's equally possible to take a stand, to say with utter determination, "Here I am, and here I will stay, until Jesus and the community life cure me." It's a real crisis.

Chapter Twenty-Six.
The First Major Crisis, Part 2

The young monk entered into his first real crisis by having to confront the self he left behind when he joined the monastery, and the self he brought along with him into the monastery. This crisis is made richer and more complex by another confrontation: with the greater self that he has made himself a part of by his entrance into the monastery—the community.

Almost inevitably, the novice imagines that in joining the community he is entering into a perfect society—perfect in both of its meanings: 1) flawless, and 2) already fully realized (*per factum*: "totally accomplished"). The dream of belonging to a perfect society is not something exclusive to monks. All of us yearn for it, and if we let go of this dream, something dies in our humanity and something withers in our vitality. But it is a dream that has to take present reality as its starting point if it is ever to come true.

The present reality of the monastic community is far from perfect. That is the social aspect of the young monk's first major crisis. Rather than being angels robed in a light and luminous vesture of human flesh, monks are earthbound creatures, often eccentric, often immature, sometimes very disrespectful of each other's human dignity, and always very different from each other.

This is not what our friend the novice was counting on. He was hoping for an assembly of venerable fathers and brothers. He was hoping for a society of unvarying courtesy, habitual charity, constant magnanimity—a community that would be a perpetual source of edification and that would merit his ever-increasing admiration. Something in him really believed that the monastery would be heaven.

And it isn't. Any monk with a number of years under his belt can tell you endless anecdotes about the surprising human defects of his fellow monks. Nothing extraordinary—and therein lies the rub. The novice was searching for a society of extraordinary men, men utterly transformed by years of prayer and the monastic routine, and here they are, no different from my father, my uncles, my cousins, my neighbors. What sense does it make to belong to a monastery if you end up no different from anybody else? Those who were meant to transform me have themselves remained remarkably resistant to transformation. One thinks of Elijah's prayer for a sudden death (Elijah, by the way, is a classical reference for monks, one of the great Old Testament predecessors of the monastic life): "Lord, it is enough. Take away my life. For I am no better than my fathers." "And my monastic fathers," adds the young monk with sudden bitterness, "aren't all that hot either."

Once again, the young monk is at a crossroads. He has discovered that this community is just as human as any other, just as human as his family, his parish, his country. He feels an urge to pack his knapsack and set out again, to return to the real world, where at least imperfect people don't claim to be perfect. That is one possibility. He can head out the door, either permanently disillusioned with the idea of human perfectibility or determined to search for it in another context. It could even be another monastic context. The writings of the fourth- and fifth-century Christian Desert Fathers are filled with stories of monks who tried their vocation in one monastery after another, always looking for authentic monastic community and never finding it.

Yes, he can walk out the door. Or he can sit down, silence his hurt feelings, look around him at the members of his community, and try to understand. Up to now, he assumed he knew what was going on in a monastery. Now, if he has the patience and humility, he can try to understand. "It is good to wait in silence for the salvation of the Lord" (Lam 3:26).

William of Saint-Thierry, friend and fellow monk of Saint Bernard, writes in his book of *Meditations* of an experience that made him feel he was seeing double. Sometimes when he looked at God, he saw simply the divine unity; at other times, gazing at the same God, he perceived a Trinity of persons. Something similar happens to the young monk looking with a pacified spirit at his community. He sees (and can never unsee, for the truth can never be unlearned) all the imperfections of his brethren. But as he keeps looking, he sees another picture, equally real, equally profound, perhaps more so: his community is a community of the beatitudes.

In the first place, it is a community of the poor in spirit. It is no surprise to the brothers that they are imperfect. They have known and accepted it for years. Nor were they trying to pull the wool over the novice's eyes. They were simply being themselves in their poverty. He just wasn't ready to see it yet. They are penetrated with an awareness of being less Christian, less faithful followers of Jesus, than they truly wish to be.

For this reason, they are a community of those who mourn. "My sin is ever before me," as it says in the great psalm of repentance, the *Miserere* (Ps 51:5). Their imperfections are a source of grief and a source of hope, at the same time. As Saint Bernard says, our misery is a magnet for God's mercy (*Steps of Humility and Pride*).

The brothers are also meek. Having permanently sacrificed their illusion of being better than others, they are gentle with their fellow sinners. It is not a false tolerance: You let me sin in my way, and I'll let you sin in yours. Rather, it is mutual compassion, in accord with the already cited recommendation of Saint Benedict: "supporting with the greatest patience one another's weaknesses of body or behavior" (RB 72:5).

Likewise, they have a "hunger and thirst for justice"—for holiness. Even though they have learned by experience that progress in the virtues is very arduous and very slow, with the constant possibility of recidivism, they keep striving to grow in prayer, in charity, in self-discipline, in silence, in obedience. (My own monks say obedience is the toughest challenge of all. That could have to do with their superior.)

The monks are merciful. In the Sermon on the Mount, mercy is more than a sentiment. It is action, is coming to the aid of those in need, whatever their need may be. The young monk perceives in the midst of eccentricities and ill-humor many gestures of fraternal charity, many acts of delicacy, many occasions when one brother carries the burden of another.

Are the brothers pure in heart? Well, they are on the way. If the young monk has a lot of patience, he will witness over the years a transformation in the faces and the gestures and the words of his brothers. There is a light and a lightness in them. Gravity is giving way to grace, as Simone Weil would say. And the source of these softened expressions and thoughtful actions is the Holy Spirit, working in the heart of the brothers, conforming their hearts to Christ, bit by bit, over a lifetime.

Not all the brothers arrive at being peacemakers, but some do. Not arbitrators, not mediators, but peacemakers. Their presence transmits peace; their smile produces peace. When they come into a room in the monastery, you don't want to keep arguing with the brother who was annoying you. Their peace is infectious.

"By patient endurance, you will save your souls," our Lord says in the Gospel (Luke 21:19). The young monk who has had patience to live through his disappointment with the imperfections of the community has saved his vocation. He has come to see that imperfection and beatitude can coexist in a single community. In fact, they always do. Saint Bernard himself had an experience of double vision. Sometimes looking at the crucifix in his cell, he saw Christ crowned with thorns; at other times, looking at the same crucifix, he saw Christ glorified. Every Christian community is both crucified and glorified, "crucified in its weakness, alive by the power of God" (2 Cor 13:4). If the young monk receives the grace to contemplate the twofold face of his community, he is on the way out of his crisis—and into a much more realistic commitment to and with his brothers.

Chapter Twenty-Seven. For Our Good and the Good of All His Holy Church

Although silence is still highly honored and well-observed in Trappist monasteries today, each monastery has a few corners where the brothers are able to have a brief chat between one monastic activity and another. During my novitiate, the favorite place for us beginners to exchange a few words was the Novices' Change Room, the place where we changed from our habit into coveralls and boots before going off in groups to manual labor. Sometimes the quality of what was said was not particularly memorable. At other times, however, there were real nuggets of gold in what we said to each other, especially when someone repeated a word of practical wisdom that he had recently heard from an older member of the community. Two of the sentences that still stick with me thirty years later have to do with motivation—the reasons for entering monastic life and the reasons for persevering in it. The two sayings go as follows: 1) Time puts our motivations to the test, and 2) Nobody stays in the monastery for the reasons for which he entered it.

The first great crisis, of which we spoke in the last two chapters, did in fact put the young monk's motivations to the test. He was forced to see how much self-love was involved in his vocational choice, how much he wanted to be a perfect monk in a perfect community. He was forced to see that much of his anguish at his imperfections did not stem from contrition at having offended God, but from disappointment at having offended himself. Likewise, that much of his irritation at the shortcomings of the community was not the fruit of holy zeal (he has discovered that he is no Elijah and no John the Baptist) but stemmed from a sense of being fooled and cheated and lured into a covenant with the mediocre. The first crisis, in short, taught him, beyond all doubt, that neither he nor the community was perfect—and that perhaps perfection is not the right reason for entering a monastery.

With this we arrive at the second piece of change-room wisdom: nobody stays in the monastery for the same reasons for which he entered. Those initial reasons were too flimsy, too self-centered, too distant from the Gospel. The young monk realizes that when Jesus said in the Sermon on the Mount, "Be perfect as your heavenly Father is perfect" (Matt 5:48), he must have been thinking of some other kind of perfection than the one the novice was pursuing and that has just been shot to pieces.

So the novice goes back to his New Testament and rereads this affirmation of Jesus, this time paying careful attention to the context. He finds that the perfection that Jesus is talking about is a Hebraic one and not a neoplatonic one, and he understands that Hebraic perfections are always relational and not individualistic. When Jesus commands us to be perfect, he is not ordering us to be flawless in our individual selves. Instead, he is ordering us to be "complete"—*shalem*—a word that has exactly the same three-letter root as the Hebrew word for peace: *Shalom*. The God of Jesus is *shalem* because his affection and concern go out to each and every person, regardless of merit: the grateful and the ungrateful, the faithful and the unfaithful, the just and the unjust. Upon them all he makes his sun to shine and his rain to fall. "And you too, my friend the novice," Jesus says to the young monk as he is doing his *lectio divina*, "You go and do likewise. Go and be *shalem* as my Father is *shalem*."

Now here is a different motivation for persevering in the monastic life, one that has surprisingly little to do with oneself as one's own work of art, one's own scientific experiment. Be complete by making the sun and rain of the heavenly Father arrive at their universal destiny. Be complete by being a channel of the Father's grace for other people. But don't get too involved in focusing on yourself as a channel. Otherwise you'll be back at square one, all absorbed in the contemplation of yourself and your indispensable role in world history. Concentrate on what you are channeling (divine grace) and to whom you are channeling (the entire human community). And let somebody else concentrate on you, the channel in the middle. Don't worry: there's no way you can fall through the cracks of the heavenly Father's loving concern. The hairs of your head are all numbered, and not a single sparrow falls to the ground without the heavenly Father knowing and caring.

If this new motivation really begins to take root, a significant shift of attention will occur. Without ceasing to be fundamentally faithful to the ascetic practices, the young monk will find his attention being more and more magnetized by the Divine Office and above all by the Eucharist. Both of them will be strangely metamorphosed for him. Previously, the Divine Office was essentially a means for experiencing religious feelings, spiritual intuitions, contemplative insights, and deep, warm silences. Now he understands that in the psalms and prayers of the Divine Office, all the needs and aspirations of humanity are contained and directed through Christ to the heavenly Father. And he, the novice, has been asked by God (this is what a vocation is) to give explicit voice to people's yearnings, concerns, sufferings, and exultation. Night and day, from Vigils to Compline, he is to stand in the divine presence, expressing with his voice, his attention, his involvement, even his bodily effort what men and women throughout the world want to say to God. He does not imagine that they are incapable of speaking for themselves, but he wants to put himself alongside them, to speak in their favor—most simply put, he wants to *pray* for them. And he knows that this is what people truly expect of him. Here in Novo Mundo, in front of our church, we have a book where our visitors can write their prayer requests. Obviously these requests are addressed principally to God; only he can answer prayers. Yet at the same time they are directed to the community: "Remember me when you stand in the presence of the Lord."

What I said about the transformation of the Divine Office is even more true with regard to the Eucharist. Before the shakeup of the crisis, the novice's Eucharist was made up of the transcendent glory of the consecration and the mystical experience of sacramental communion. Not that there is anything reprehensible in being especially moved by these two key moments in the liturgy.

The problem was not in the experience of God's grandeur and God's intimacy. It was in the *narrowness* of the experience. The young monk was living a private Mass. Whether anybody else was in the monastic church was irrelevant (as long as they didn't make noise). Mass was for *him*, for his immersion in the divine mystery through the transubstantiation of the bread and wine and his own transubstantiation into Christ.

Now he hears loud and clear the invitation of the celebrant at the beginning of the Eucharistic prayer, and he hears—and understands—the response of the community, of which he is a part: "The Lord receive the sacrifice at your hands, for the praise and glory of his name, for our good and the good of all his holy Church." *All* his holy Church. The young monk perceives that the Mass is ecclesial, and to the extent he does so, he himself becomes ecclesial. He sees that there is apostolic work to be done in consequence of his reception of Christ's body and blood. As Saint Edith Stein said in her meditation *Ave, Spes Unica*, "In the power of the blood of Christ, the contemplative is able to be in all places at once—soothing, healing, helping." Receiving communion is now the key to the monk's mission of loving intercessory prayer. Things have changed. His reasons for staying are truly different than his reasons for coming. "Behold," says the Lord. "I make all things new." Including motivations.

Chapter Twenty-Eight. "From Now On I Will Be with You Forever"

Athanasius's *Life of Anthony* alternates between dramatic battles between Anthony and the Evil One and tranquil classes in ascetic doctrine administered by Anthony to his disciples. The first truly dramatic scene occurs soon after Anthony decides to embrace the monastic life. He has recently moved from the outskirts of his hometown into solitude. In fact, he is living in an abandoned tomb, to make it as clear as possible that through the power of the Risen Christ he intends to confront and conquer death and the devil. The demon takes up Anthony's challenge, and Anthony ends up getting more than he expected. He is beaten within an inch of his life. In fact, his friends who come to visit him think that they have found a cadaver instead of a living human being. They bring him back to town to prepare him for burial.

Amazingly, Anthony not only recovers consciousness but hastens back to the tomb to renew the struggle, from which he emerges victorious. The battle concluded, the tomb is suddenly filled with a great supernatural light, which Anthony immediately recognizes as the presence of the glorified Christ. He does not kneel in adoration, however. A little disgruntled that he had to do all the fighting single-handed, he complains to Christ, "Where were you when I needed you, Lord?" Or, in other words, "It's sure nice to see you, but I would have appreciated it even more if you had been here to help me when I was in serious trouble." Jesus regards Anthony's attitude as understandable and does not take it as a sign of disrespect. But he explains to Anthony that the situation is not exactly as Anthony has described it: "I *was* here the whole time, Anthony, observing your contest. And after having seen that it truly is your intention to persevere in the monastic struggle, I promise you, from now on I will be with you forever."

This incident of the nighttime wrestling match with the demon in the tombs is the primordial version of the great novitiate crisis that we have been reflecting on in the last few chapters. In Anthony's case, the drama is presented in intensely physical and sensorial terms: the dreadfulness of the cemetery, the darkness of the night, the complete isolation from other people, the bodily attack that comes close to ending Anthony's life, the undeniable presence of the Evil One communicated by loud noises and shrieks, the revelation of Christ's presence through a supernatural light that illuminates the tomb. All these aspects are, at first glance, very different from the experience of a typical novice put to the test in the context of a monastic community. Actually, however, the trial of Anthony is essentially the same as that of a novice of the twenty-first century. Athanasius has translated an essentially interior occurrence into visual and auditory terms and in so doing has made it unforgettable for the reader. But in its core the trial of Anthony in Egypt and the trial of a novice in Campo do Tenente are one and the same. Through it, each of them discovers the role of Christ in the monastic warfare.

In the highly psychological culture to which we belong, people are continuously aware of themselves, their personal efforts, and their individual growth processes. In the monastery too it is possible to focus almost entirely on one's personal fidelity, on the difficulty of dedicating oneself day after day to the spiritual endeavor, on the wear and tear that this causes to the emotions. It could even be that the monastery, as a place that demands so much effort, constantly and not intermittently, constitutes an environment more prone to make its members conscious of their involvement in their own development. It cannot be a mere accident that the heresy of Pelagianism, which overemphasizes the part played by human initiative to the detriment of God's grace, found its greatest defenders in the ascetics of the desert. Cassian himself, despite the immense influence he exerted on the doctrine of Saints Benedict, Bernard, Dominic, Ignatius Loyola, and John of the Cross, never came to be officially considered a saint in the Western Church but only a "blessed," precisely because some of his affirmations were considered semi-Pelagian.

In other words, there is a very strong tendency in the novice of our times, as there was in Anthony himself, to experience the monastic trials as a solitary endeavor, to imagine that he is going it alone. Certainly before the crisis, he had hoped that Christ would be there to aid him in the hour of trial, and that the two of them would be fighting side by side. But apparently when the devil came through the door of the tomb, Christ went out the window. It is almost as if he were a kind of Saint Peter during the time of our passion. "Father Bernard?" (I'll use myself as an example), Jesus says to the Evil One as he is about to attack me. "No, never heard of him. Sorry. Catch you later."

What Anthony learns from Christ at the conclusion of his first great moment of combat is that this impression of abandonment is totally unjustified. Christ was never absent from his struggle, not even for an instant. He was present the whole time.

To us it may seem mysterious and even irritating that Christ explains to Anthony that in the hour of conflict he chose to be present as an observer rather than as a fellow combatant. If this is our impression, we do not fully grasp the meaning of this incident. On the one hand, the devil is putting Anthony to the test with the intention of either destroying him or making him desist from the monastic undertaking. But Christ is likewise putting Anthony to the test. Obviously, his intentions are very different. Destruction and discouragement are far from his mind. Yet he *does* want to put Anthony to the proof. He *does* want to test Anthony's mettle, to find out if he is absolutely determined to belong to him and to be a genuine witness of his resurrection. As the Wisdom literature of the Old Testament makes clear, this attitude on God's part is not something new. Every person that God desires to have as his friend has to pass through an experience like this. And God is neither absent nor indifferent. Rather, he is watching—and waiting—and hoping—and rooting for us. He, more than anyone, wants Anthony to come through victorious, victorious through the power of divine grace—which for the moment he chooses to leave invisible.

Then comes the best part. Anthony has passed the test, with flying colors. And Christ, who was a royal observer of Anthony's struggle, seated in the imperial box while Anthony sweated in the arena, now swears eternal fidelity to him as his friend and helper. However great the difficulties Anthony may have to face in the future, in the core of his soul, he will always know that Christ is alongside him: "My rock, who trains my arms for battle, my hands for war" (Ps 144:1). Does the novice of our day and age have the experience of being formally and solemnly received by Christ as companion, of being partner with Christ in a covenant of friendship? Yes, he does, and for this reason no other subsequent crisis is as grueling as this first one. The final words of Christ to his disciples, "I am with you always to the end of time" (Matt 28:20), have become personal truth for him. In this sense, it is impossible to talk of a totally eremitic life in the Christian tradition. The light that shone from the roof of the tomb, the light of Christ, the light that is Christ, has penetrated the monk's heart. Christ is the mysterious but utterly real companion in the monk's cell. From now on, they have everything in common.

Chapter Twenty-Nine.
The Years of Simple Profession

Over the centuries, the period between entrance into the monastery and definitive commitment to monastic life—solemn profession—has grown ever longer. In the time of the first desert monks (third and fourth centuries), entrance into the community itself constituted the decisive step. From the day on which you renounced the world to become a monk, you had bound yourself forever to this new way of life. "No one who has put his hand to the plow and looks back is worthy of the kingdom of God." These words of Jesus from the gospel of Luke (Luke 9:62) translate the attitude of the earliest monks with regard to the coincidence of entrance into the monastery and permanent commitment.

By the time of Saint Benedict in the sixth century, the situation had changed significantly. His Rule clearly mandates a year of monastic experience prior to the assumption of a definitive and perpetual obligation. On the one hand, this change on the part of Benedict must have been the fruit of his characteristic tendency towards moderation and the avoidance of all kinds of extremism. On the other, the introduction of a one-year novitiate probably indicates that as a matter of fact many young entrants did not persevere in the monastic endeavor. Saint Benedict's decision to add a period of probation prior to vows corresponds to an intuition from the book of Ecclesiastes: "Better not to make vows than to make them and not fulfill them" (Eccl 5:4). Benedict structured the novitiate year in such a way that by the time the year of probation came to an end the novice really knew what he was getting into. He knew from a year of intense experience what the yoke of the Rule consisted of. He had passed through many emotional ups and downs and had discovered for himself what it means to live day after day a form of life marked by obedience, fidelity to the Divine Office, and trials of every kind. He had had the Rule read to him in its entirety a number of times in the course of the year of initiation, so there was no doubt as to the nature of the responsibilities he was assuming. The whole year had been a period of extended reflection. And now he was ready to decide if he wished to take on the yoke of the Rule or not.

Things remained thus until the beginning of the twentieth century. The Code of Canon Law of 1917 introduced an extension of the time of formation and discernment between the novitiate and the emission of solemn vows. This period was called simple or temporary profession, or here in Brazil triennial profession, because three years is the minimum time of temporary vows and is most frequently the amount of time a young monk passes between his first vows and his solemn ones. Nevertheless, the actual Code of Canon Law makes provision for up to nine years of simple vows prior to the definitive commitment. How many years a person will spend as a "temporarily professed" depends on a double discernment—his own personal one and the discernment of the community.

We can flesh out the quotation from the Book of Ecclesiastes: "You are on the way to embracing forever a difficult and demanding form of life. You will, through a richly symbolic and theologically profound liturgical ceremony, say before God, his saints, and the Church that you will be faithful to this form of life—this *conversatio*—until death. Be careful, then, that you are resolved with every fiber of your being to stand firm in your promises. If you have not yet reached this level of conviction, it is better to wait than to proceed rashly." And proceeding rashly is not something that can be measured chronologically. Proceeding rashly means asking to make solemn vows before you have reached the moral certainly that this is God's will for you and your will for yourself.

If you add up the time spent as a candidate, the three-month observership, the six months of postulancy (at least six months), the two years of novitiate—at some point the time of the novitiate was doubled in our Order from one year to two—and the nine-year maximum foreseen for simple profession, one can spend up to fifteen years discerning one's monastic vocation. What a phenomenal change from the practice of the Desert Fathers!

And yet the mere passage of time and the mere accumulation of experience will never be sufficient to lead a person to a vocational clarity sufficient to justify the request to be admitted to solemn vows. What, then, is the purpose of temporary profession? What is gained by inserting years of deliberation between the vows at the end of novitiate and perpetual vows? The answer that has formulated itself in my own mind over the years can be expressed by two Portuguese words, similar to each other in sound and probably at one time in meaning as well, but now significantly different. The two words are *capricho*—caprice—and *caprichar*—to give your best to some undertaking. The key question for the simply professed monk is, "Are you going to give yourself to the *conversatio* by *capricho* or are you going to *caprichar* in your dedication to it?"

To be a monk by *capricho* is to throw yourself into the life when the mood strikes you, participating actively in the Divine Office when you're feeling enthused, working with diligence when you've had a good night's sleep, praying the Scriptures when they show themselves to be immediately interesting, collaborating with those brothers that you find it easy to be with, praying the rosary on the basis of a sudden, inexplicable inspiration, and so on. To be a monk who decides once and for all to *caprichar* is to dedicate yourself to the monastic life with the same generosity and the same fidelity every day and in every situation. To put it in another way, the self-gift of the truly dedicated monk does not depend on the inclination of the moment but on a firm and stable decision taken before God to use to the utmost the liberty that God has given him do what is right and just whatever the circumstances: affective, interpersonal, communitarian, physical, spiritual (the well-known alternation between consolation and desolation, between experiencing the Lord as present or as absent). This is the monk who has attained the quality of being *semper idem*, consistently faithful to himself and to the state of life he has embraced.

It is this movement from oscillation to steadiness that should take place during the years of simple profession, and that will be the making or the breaking of the monk. If someone is unable to transcend his moods and whims, little by little he will discover that the inclination to devote himself wholeheartedly to the monastic endeavor will become increasingly rare. The moments of enthusiasm will become fewer and fewer, the times that he experiences himself as happy in his vocation will diminish, the sensation of being condemned to a monastic vocation will come to dominate more and more. This is because, fundamentally, *capricho* and monastic life are radically opposed.

Monastic life was never meant to be lived, and never can be lived, on the basis of warm feelings. Monastic life is a fierce and humble determination to be faithful to grace and to spend oneself every day and all day out of the abundant graces that the Holy Spirit bestows on us. More clearly still: one of the chief goals of monastic life is to transfer us from an existence based on the feelings of the moment to an existence that operates out of a clear and enlightened intellect and a strong will habitually inclined to the good. In *Stages on Life's Way* Kierkegaard spoke of a fully human existence as being comprised of the movement from the aesthetic (based on feelings) to the moral (based on conviction) to the theological (based on direct contact with God and his will). The years of simple profession have as their goal the move from the aesthetic to the moral.

Should someone not make this important move during the years of simple profession, there remain two possible outcomes: either he will leave the monastery (the more frequent decision) or he will carry into solemn profession a great task that he should have accomplished before making final vows. Jesus says, "Sufficient to the day is the evil thereof" (Matt 6:34). We were not made to work at two major challenges at the same time; that is too much for our frail shoulders. Much to be preferred is to take advantage of the years of temporary profession in order to truly internalize the value of stability, where stability does not simply mean continuing to have your street address at the monastery but rather a fixed and ever renewed and implemented decision to live according to God's Word and the Rule of Saint Benedict. To "live by faith and not by feelings" is strong medicine in the beginning, but it ultimately shows itself as the only way to become a genuinely faithful monk and a genuinely happy one as well.

Chapter Thirty. Solemn Profession

Many years ago, I was struck by a passage from the book *Spiritual Exercises: A Retreat for Priests* by the great Jesuit theologian Karl Rahner. Rahner says that God most clearly shows his respect for our human liberty by permitting us to write our life in ink rather than with pencil. A life written in pencil would be a provisory life, a life where nothing is definitive, in which every act that is posited, no matter how serious or how sublime, could always be erased afterwards, if people should happen to change their minds. Nothing would be permanent: the eraser could be depended upon to effectively undo whatever didn't fit in anymore with a person's new plans.

Rahner insists that even if we ourselves prefer the security of sketching in pencil, God and reality (or better still, God who is Reality) read our writing in another way. As God sees it, we human beings *are* capable of definitive acts, of making stable and unchanging commitments. We were created capable of assuming responsibility for our decisions and actions. We were created capable of lifelong fidelity to our deepest choices and accepting all the consequences that flow from them. This is our greatness. We can genuinely commit ourselves; we can declare ourselves fully and never go back on our word. Another way of saying this: we human beings are able to enter into a covenant with another— with God, with a community, with another person—"a new and eternal covenant," as Jesus describes his own deepest and most radical decision. We can posit an act that is "forever." This is our glory—even if we tremble before it.

The definitive act in the making of a monk—the act that truly makes him a monk—is his solemn profession. Through this act, a monk gives himself away. He entrusts his entire life to God, to the monastic way of life, and to his community. No longer does he promise to live the vows for one year as in the period of simple profession. Now he promises to live them until death. He has recognized that what matters for him above all else is to strive to live the first and greatest of all the commandments: "You shall love the Lord your God with all your heart, with all your soul, with all your mind, and with all your strength" (Mark 12:29-30). Through solemn profession he promises with the utmost seriousness that he will employ all the resources of his inward self—heart, soul, mind, strength—for this unique and exclusive aim: to love God. Furthermore, he promises that he will realize this fidelity in a very particular and concrete way: through the specificity of the monastic life in all its essential values and practices, as a member of a particular, highly distinct community and in obedience to a spiritual guide, the abbot. Over the course of many years, from candidacy through postulancy through novitiate through temporary profession, the monk in formation has discovered what Saint Ignatius of Loyola termed the *id quod volo*: what it is that I most truly and wholeheartedly desire. He has learned beyond a doubt that it is God himself, and now he takes the step that totally orients him to the fulfillment of his desire.

Having said all this, the question remains: Where do monks and nuns get the courage to definitively offer themselves to God in this way? They have had so much experience of their own human frailty in the course of their years in the monastery. They have come face to face, time and again, with the instability of their desires, with their incapacity to live unwaveringly fixed on God. They remember how many times they have thought of knocking on the abbot's or abbess's door to communicate, politely but firmly, their decision: "My bags are packed." Certainly they are not naïve enough to believe that a lifetime commitment will of itself resolve and eliminate all future ambiguity. They have not thrown themselves into solemn vows simply to cut off all possibility of return. But then, what gives them the confidence to offer their whole life in this kind of perpetual oblation?

If this thought has already occurred to you—"How could anyone possibly make this sort of gift of self?"—I congratulate you. It is a very sensible question. All we monks make it too, especially the night before our solemn vows. The answer is that although we habitually speak of a ceremony of solemn profession, when we do so, we are in fact abbreviating. Two inseparable acts—two acts of permanent self-commitment—take place on the day of solemn profession. Were it not so, we could not speak in terms of a covenant.

The first part of the liturgy of vows does consist of the brothers' promise of perpetual fidelity to God in the monastic vocation. This is their *professio*: their profession of faith and their profession of life. But they are not yet solemnly professed monks. They have made their profession; they have expressed their ultimate intention. But this oblation, to be real, must not only be made but also accepted. God must declare himself as well. The monk fully recognizes this fact, and during the ceremony of profession, immediately after having read aloud in the presence of the abbot and the community the document he wrote (in pen!) offering himself forever to God, after having signed it and given it to the abbot, who places it on the altar to be offered up together with the bread and wine of the eucharistic celebration that will soon follow, the monk sings the following words three times: "Receive me, Lord, according to your promise that I will live; do not disappoint me."

Each time he sings these words he intones them on a higher note, conveying the intensity of his petition. And after each of the three times that he makes his appeal to God to accept the offering he has made, all those present in the monastery church repeat the verse after him. So not only is the brother imploring that God deign to receive him into his service forever as a monk; the whole church of Christ, symbolically present in the members of the monastic community and in the person of family members and friends who have come to participate in this decisive moment, make appeal for him. Once the monk has asked and asked and asked a third time that God receive him, he has said all that he can say. Now he waits for an answer.

But does an answer really come? Being able to say "yes" to this question is of the greatest importance, not only as regards monastic profession but as regards all liturgy. God is not passive in liturgical celebration. He is not an idol to be implored, adored, praised, cajoled. God *acts* in the liturgical celebration. He acts and the church acts, in each of its members and as a community of faith. His action is divine and utterly spiritual and cannot be fully perceived with our ordinary senses. He acts sacramentally, but he really and truly acts.

With this we come at last to the full name of the ceremony we are describing: Monastic Profession and Consecration. Once the monk has professed his intention and appealed to God to accept and confirm the action he has just realized, the monk kneels before the abbot, who pronounces a long and theologically rich consecratory prayer, with his hands imposed on the head of the monk. The abbot, who, in the words of the Holy Rule, "holds the place of Christ in the monastery," invokes each of the Divine Persons one by one—Father, Son, and Holy Spirit—asking them to come and purify the heart of the monk, forgive him all his sins, strengthen him in his resolve, make him whole-hearted and unrestricted in his self-giving, and, above all, asking them to assent to and ratify the covenant that the monk knows himself called to.

If you remember the story of Elijah on Mount Carmel, when he asked the God of Israel to accept the holocaust that he had placed on the wood over the stone altar that he himself had fashioned and God in response descended from heaven in fire, consuming the holocaust, the wood, and the altar stones and licking up the water that had been poured into the trench, then you have the key to understanding monastic consecration. The abbot is like Elijah; the kneeling monk is the holocaust, over which the prophet poured water in abundance to show that "for God nothing is impossible," and God is the fire. Having had the privilege to preside as abbot at a good number of solemn professions, I know with utter certainty that at this moment God does come down as spiritual fire, as the fire of the Spirit, and passes through my hands onto the head of the monk as I rest my hands upon it and from there fills and ignites his whole being. God has spoken, hidden but genuinely present in the prayer of consecration, and now it can be said (as Jesus said of himself): *Consummatum est*. The holocaust has been accepted. The new covenant has been realized. God and this monk have been fused together in the fire of a divine and a human love.

Chapter Thirty-One. First Steps
in Spiritual Fatherhood

In his great commentary on the Song of Songs, Saint Bernard says that the infused gift of the Holy Spirit not only intimately unites the soul to Christ but also makes her pregnant, gives her the charism of spiritual maternity, the responsibility to nurture and educate beginners in the spiritual life and help them arrive at their maturity (SC 9.2).

Something analogous can be said with regard to the solemn profession of monks and nuns. The consecration that they receive contains a power intended for more than their own personal sanctification. It is meant to be used for the upbuilding of the church, and in particular of the local church that is their monastic community. On the same day that God accepts the holocaust of their solemn profession, God begins to transform the monk or nun into a spiritual father or a spiritual mother, a father or mother of souls—the plenitude of the monastic vocation.

What are the ways by which a young solemnly professed enters into this paternity or maternity? Certainly the first and most decisive step is the acceptance of this new identity. If before profession the monks' and nuns' growth consisted in the gradual and profound assimilation of the words of Saint Paul, "For me to live is Christ" (Phil 1:21), their new motto must now be *Pro Christo et Ecclesia*—to live for Christ and the Church. Christ must continue to increase in them, but they must recognize that the abundance of the Christ-life within them should not be grasped as a private treasure but made available every day to all the members of the community. To cite another idea of Saint Bernard: whereas novices must be careful not to prematurely give to others the waters of the Holy Spirit just beginning to flow within them, lest they leave themselves dry and empty of grace, the mature monk or nun is like the basin of a fountain that has been filled to the brim and that is meant to overflow in benefit of others. The waters of the Spirit constantly spring up within them and replenish them. They need no longer fear that in sharing the treasures of the Spirit they will leave themselves destitute (SC 18).

Concretely, how do monks and nuns go about imparting the Spirit? The most fundamental way is by assuming the responsibility of living as a true icon of the monastic vocation, above all, for those who have entered the community after them and for their peers. This can sound extremely idealistic (if not pretentious), but in fact, all solemnly professed monks and nuns exercise a tremendous influence on the community by their way of corresponding (or not corresponding) to the truth of their vocation. In our own Trappist Order, it has become clearer and clearer in the years since the Second Vatican Council that the prime formator of new monks is the community as a whole. Even though the abbot or abbess may be a charismatic figure and the novice master or mistress a "living Rule" (as they used to say in the old days), if the professed community does not embody their teaching, the two of them will only be voices in the wilderness, destined to die out amid the desert sands.

It requires a certain interior revolution to pass from being a youngster in formation whose shortcomings are accepted with a smile ("Youth must have its day") to being an adult whose daily fidelity along with that of the other solemnly professed monks and nuns constitutes the bedrock of the community. This is a genuine asceticism: to renounce the ease of being carried by the community and to assume the burden of carrying the community through the authenticity of one's witness to Christ and one's vocation. As a matter of fact, not a few young solemnly professed monks and nuns stumble a bit under this new weight. That is not a problem. All that is required is that each one learn to adapt to the new situation while becoming able to shoulder this burden with a growing naturalness.

What should help them to assume this new responsibility for accurately modeling the monastic life to their brothers and sisters, not as theater but in love and in deed, is the fact that with solemn vows monks become members of the conventual chapter. Henceforth they will be actively involved in the deliberations and decisions of major importance affecting the community. They will vote for or against the acceptance of a novice to simple vows and of a simply professed to solemn vows. They will be consulted about the suitability of a brother monk for priestly ordination. They will take part in the choice of the members of the abbot's council, of the delegates for regional meetings, of the officials within the community. Major financial decisions, decisions about construction projects, and a host of other issues require the consent of the conventual chapter to which they now belong. The privilege and the responsibility to actively participate in the outcome of all these questions, if it is to mean something more than simply an acquired right or the exercise of power, should make the young solemnly professed conscious of his or her obligation to be a holy monk. Within the monastic context, it should be impossible to separate a truly dedicated life from participation in the decision-making processes of the community.

Another significant surprise for the professed monk—another dimension of his newly acquired fatherhood—is the taking on of greater responsibilities within the community. It is almost a certainty that within the first few months after solemn profession, the abbot will invite him to his office to propose some new job to him. The proposal will have its attractive side: what person is there who does not enjoy the idea of a promotion? Soon enough, however, the promoted monk will discover that in a certain sense his new task has turned his life upside down. Frequently, it will involve working longer hours than those he worked as a novice or a simply professed. It will be the kind of work that involves a greater engagement of his intelligence and affectivity (certainly more than was necessary for sweeping the abbey church!) and that therefore cannot be immediately forgotten when one turns out the lights in the workplace. It can involve the spiritual, physical, or fiscal well-being of the community, so that mistakes or negligence can have far-reaching negative consequences not only for the person in charge but for everybody. Very often it will be the kind of demanding work that affects his digestion and his sleep patterns.

Speaking from personal experience, I can attest that up until solemn profession I was able to fall asleep within fifteen minutes after the end of the last liturgical office of the day. As novice master, prior, and finally abbot I now require at least an hour of prayer and reading to pass from the various stimulations and demands of the day to the ability to calmly fall asleep in the peace of the Lord. The solemnly professed have to learn a new way to integrate their spiritual discipline and the demands of their community assignments. It is a juggling act that can take years to master. It is not uncommon, after a few months of enthusiasm in the new job, for the young solemnly professed to request an interview with the abbot with the intention of withdrawing from the new assignment.

It is then that he will discover that while the Constitutions speak explicitly of not giving tasks to novices and juniors that could interfere with their spiritual formation, there is absolutely nothing written (not even in the small print) about protecting the solemnly professed from the weight of such labors. These are precisely the works that are reserved for the solemnly professed. Fulfilling them in peace and without sacrificing the spiritual dimension of our life can be a painful adjustment, can be a cross. Normally, however, grace, time, and good will resolve the question, and the cross of a heavy community responsibility becomes a life-giving cross.

Above all, solemnly professed monks are called upon sincerely and perceptibly to love their community. Our Cistercian Fathers often posed this question in their writings: *Quid difficile amanti?* "What can be hard for someone who loves?" There is no greater good and no greater testimony that solemnly professed can give their brothers and sisters than to be visibly in love with their own community. Whatever their shortcomings, if it is clear that they joyfully love their community, they are truly becoming spiritual fathers and mothers within it.

Chapter Thirty-Two.
The Possibility of Priesthood

Until fairly recently, when a young man presented himself at the gate of the monastery, the officials of the community had to discern before admitting him whether the candidate was called to the choir-monk vocation or the laybrother vocation. The choir-monk vocation implied a commitment to actively participating in the full choral office, which at that time meant seven or eight hours a day in church, along with an hour or so of manual labor. The laybrother vocation, on the other hand, was a call to generous manual labor, perhaps eight to ten hours of it daily, and a prayer life that basically consisted in brief periods of common prayer composed of the recitation of a certain number of Our Fathers and Hail Marys. The two vocations were considered complementary, each group feeling a merited pride in its particular version of the call to the cloistered life. Sometimes the decisive vocational question made to a candidate was, "Can you sing?"

But more was at stake than simply singing, as can be seen in the very name *laybrother*. The laybrother was a religious but not a cleric, and would never be ordained to the priesthood. The choir monks for their part were all considered as destined for the clerical state and eventually for priestly ordination. Thus the decision regarding priesthood was made before even entering the monastery. Those who came in as choir monks began their philosophical studies during the novitiate itself, and in the succeeding years the time not dedicated to the choral office was reserved for courses in philosophy and theology. Monastic formation and priestly formation were realized in tandem; ordinarily, priestly ordination followed soon after solemn profession.

All of this has changed radically, at least in our Order, since the years of Vatican II. No longer are there two distinct groups in the monastic community, choir monks and laybrothers. All who enter, enter as monks, all receive the same monastic formation, and all live a monastic day evenly divided between liturgical prayer and manual labor.

Is this to say that all become priests? On the contrary. The perception has grown in recent decades that primitive monasticism—the golden age of monasticism—was essentially a lay phenomenon. Often enough there was not a single priest in a monastic community of the early centuries, and the community would go *en masse* to the nearest parish to participate in the Sunday Eucharist. A symbolic indication of a gradually decreasing identification of the monk with the clerical state is found in the classification of Saint Benedict. Throughout the Middle Ages and up to the nineteenth century, it was more than obvious that Benedict must have been a priest. At the end of the nineteenth century, he was reassigned as a deacon. (There is a stained glass window of him vested as a deacon in one of the chapels of my first monastic community in Massachusetts.) Today the great majority of scholars are convinced that Benedict was neither priest nor deacon. According to them, our holy father Saint Benedict was in reality our holy brother Benedict. Father still, of course, in the sense of being a spiritual father, a begetter of spiritual life in the hearts of his disciples by his doctrine and example. But father as in "Father Benedict"? No.

Where does this leave a young man of 2019 who feels a call to monastic life and an equally strong call to the priesthood? It leaves him without any guarantee of future priestly ordination—something, he is told, that will be discerned only after solemn profession—and it leaves him with the obligation to consecrate himself totally to growing into his identity as a monk. As far as intellectual formation is concerned, the years of initial formation are oriented almost entirely to monastic studies. What the novice and junior professed study are the Scriptures, the Rule, the writings of the Fathers of the Desert and the medieval monastic writers, monastic values and monastic practices, the psalms, the practice of *lectio divina*, the liturgical year, the practice of interior prayer.

All of these are "studies" in the original sense of the Latin word. They are objects of effort and application that the novice devotes himself to for no other reason than to become a monk. He does not attend classes on prayer so that one day he can teach other people how to pray, but so that one day, by the mercy of God, he may become a man of prayer. He does not study the sacraments so as one day to be able intelligently to administer the sacraments. Rather he studies the sacraments because to be a baptized, confirmed, and "eucharistized" human being is at the center of his identity as it is meant to be at the center of the identity of every Christian. If there is anything pastoral about his monastic studies up to the time of solemn profession, it is that he is being formed by Christ, the pastor of the whole Christian flock, as a genuine sheep of his pasture.

But to return to the question of the preceding paragraph: what about the monk in formation who is convinced of a call both to the monastic life and to the ministerial priesthood? Actually, his situation is not so difficult as it seems. In the first place, the present policy delivers him from an automatic priesthood, a priesthood that in the old dispensation was part of the uniform monastic package, and that was not universally desired or profoundly appropriated. Second, during his first years in the community, he gets to receive a clear and solid grounding in his monastic vocation. This prepares him to confront head-on and in a fully informed way *the* essential question: "Do I want to be a monk?" without its being diluted or confused by his engaging in seminary studies at the same time that he is meant to be immersed in the work of acquiring a monastic identity.

Third, the long deferment of the fulfillment of his desire to be a priest should serve to test and purify his motivation. As Saint Gregory the Great wrote in his *Homilies on the Gospels*, "All holy desires grow by delay. If they do not grow, they were never truly holy desires" (Homily 25). Fourth, he comes to perceive that in the context of the enclosed monastic life, there is relatively little opportunity for ministerial activity. Unless he happens to be chosen by the abbot as guest master, he will not have much occasion to do pastoral counseling. He will almost never baptize, marry, or anoint the sick. He will hear confessions only if the brothers choose him freely as their confessor—a wonderful stimulus for living in peace and charity with his brethren in the community. (No monk of our day and age is going to let himself be forced to go to confession with Father Sourpuss.) He will give a full-length homily perhaps every two months, depending on the number of priests in the community, who usually take turns being "hebdom-adary"—the presider of the liturgy for the week. All that he is sure of, so to speak, is that if he is ordained, every day he will celebrate or concelebrate the Eucharist with and for his community.

By divine providence, it can happen that it is exactly this possibility of celebrating the Eucharist that is at the heart of a monk's desire to be a priest. The young monk is a fervent disciple of Christ and seeks for the way to become as close to him—as one with him—as possible. The way to his objective, he intuits, is the Eucharist. It is not that he doubts the intimacy with Christ that is bestowed on all Christians who participate in the sacraments. As a baptized Christian and religious, he has already lived that intimacy for many years; it is the experiential basis of his present desire. Nonetheless, something in his heart tells him that there exists a nearer access to Christ, perhaps not necessary for everyone, but personally necessary for him. He wants to be united to Christ in his character as high priest and as holocaust. He wants to offer Christ to the Father and to be offered in Christ to the Father. He perceives what might be described as a third kind of priesthood, alongside the priesthood of all the faithful, and the ministerial priesthood: a mystical priesthood founded on an intense communion and identification with Christ in offering the sacrifice of the Mass. All readers, according to their theology and spirituality, can judge whether such a perception is legitimate. I think it is.

And while you're evaluating, please pray for our community. God willing, we'll be ordaining a few more monastic priests over the next few years.

Chapter Thirty-Three.
God Gives the Growth

In the last act of Shakespeare's great tragedy *King Lear*, one of the principal characters asserts, "Ripeness is all" (Act 5, Scene 2). All that matters is that the plant, the animal, and especially the human being arrive at his or her God-intended fullness, reach the beauty, the maturity, the goodness, and the wisdom that God implanted at creation and that he has nourished and cultivated throughout the creature's lifetime. The good seed is the word of God; the good soil in which he sows it is we ourselves.

From its beginnings, Benedictine monasticism has been associated with agriculture. Along with the church, the refectory, the chapter room, and the scriptorium, there is a fifth place of instruction in the monastery: the fields. The fields are a tremendously expressive parable of what the monastic life is about: being planted, growing, ripening, and being harvested. The monks or nuns who work in the fields (and even those who do not, but walk through them in their free time) see their own life revealed and mirrored in what is going on in the soil. They feel an instinctive kinship with what is happening out there, because they recognize that the same process is taking place in here, that is, in the heart and mind, and, yes, in the body as well.

Up until now, in these reflections on "The Making of a Monk," we have been looking at the time of planting: the emergence of the shoot from the earth and the appearance of that singular shade of green, in stalk or leaf, that belongs particularly to spring: springtime green. All this time we have been talking about beginnings. I remember that at the end of my years of my initial formation, my junior master wrote an evaluation before recommending

me for solemn vows. In order to compose his report he had inter-
viewed all the sixty solemnly professed monks of the community
and synthesized their intuitions and opinions. One afternoon, we
read the text together. The final sentence was, "In conclusion,
there is reason to hope that in fifteen or twenty years, Bernard
may turn out to be a good monk." I was furious. "Fifteen or twenty
years!" I said, all choked up. "I have spent the last five years giving every ounce of myself to the monastic endeavor, and all they
have to say is that in fifteen or twenty years, I might turn out to
be a good monk!" "Bernard," my junior master said. "They are
wiser than you and have much more experience. They know that
nobody can become a good monk in five years. He can show
promise, yes, but there's an awful lot that has to happen, over the
course of many years, before someone can truly become a monk
at all, good, bad, or indifferent. Actually, they were trying to com-
pliment you." I have to say that at the time I didn't feel myself
very complimented. I felt very underappreciated. Thirty years
later, I have come to see that they were right.

What has helped me a lot in coming to this conclusion is our
soybeans (our chief crop, along with wheat, as it is for so many
farmers in southern Brazil). I will never forget my first autumn
here in the state of Paraná, the autumn of 1997. In January and
February—not yet autumn—I looked in joy and admiration at the
acres of vibrant green plants. "Surely, they are ready to be harvested" (you have to keep in my mind that I was born and bred
in New York City). In February, the green started to mutate into
gold, the closest I have seen in Brazil to the changing of the leaves
in the northern hemisphere in October. I had to admit that the
transformation was glorious. The green had been vitality itself,
but the gold was pure magnificence. "Surely, *now* is the time for
the harvest." But nobody made a move to harvest anything. I began
to be preoccupied when the glorious gold slowly faded to a
brown, and a drier brown, and then an extremely dry brown. The
plants had become completely desiccated. As far as I could interpret, it was all death and loss. And then, a few weeks later, some
of the monks and our field hands went out with the machinery
and began to harvest. "Harvest what?" I asked myself. "Harvest
the soybeans, finally ready to be harvested." The soybeans were
a book of wisdom.

I'm not sure if Saint Bernard ever saw a soybean, but he has a brief text on spiritual growth that makes me think that maybe he did: "In the beginning, the spiritual life is sweet but superficial, then it is dry but extremely nourishing, and finally it is simple and delightful." Having made so many mistakes in my life, I stand to be corrected here as well, but it seems to me that the longest part of the process, the major part of the process, is the middle, when things are "dry but nourishing."

Dry doesn't necessarily imply painful, merely a process that is slow, steady, and without much excitement, a process that changes our leaves from green to gold to brown. In his commentary on the Song of Songs, reflecting on the verse, *Nigra sum, sed formosa*—"I am dark but beautiful"—Origen explains that the dark complexion of the bride, the soul intimately united with the Lord, is the result of her years of long exposure to the rays of Christ, her sun. He teaches that it is precisely this exposure that is the central dynamic in the spiritual life: to live warmed and bronzed and burnt by the heat and the brightness of Christ. I paraphrase him: "Make sure you stand and keep standing directly under the rays of the sun. If you stand off at an angle, you won't absorb the full strength of Christ's rays, and he won't be able to warm and form you into his perfect likeness. Stand right under the sun and don't move. The darker you become, the more Christlike you are becoming." "If anything," Origen continues, "the verse should read, 'I am black *and* beautiful.' I am beautiful because I am black. I am beautiful because I have allowed Christ to dye me and tint me with all the force of his divinity."

That is basically what we do in the long middle years of the monastic life. We seek to live in the presence of God, and to stay put in it. In the beginning, we needed to become aware that there really is a presence of God in the world—that he is eternally present to all things (this Saint Benedict calls the first step of humility). Then we had to practice this presence—jog our memory many times in the course of a day, in order to not forget that we live in God's presence, in order not to slip back into forgetfulness. But a time comes when this presence has become a stable presence in our lives, has become *the* stable presence in our lives, and then we see that what life is all about is to persevere in this presence. The Carmelites, who consider the prophet Elijah as their true founder, love to cite his words as a resumé of the spiritual quest: "As the Lord lives, *in whose presence I stand*" (1 Kgs 17:11). All the fathers of the church point out the relationship between the word *stand* and the word *stability*. To "stand in the presence of the Lord" does not mean to expose yourself to it twenty minutes a day, on the days that you remember. It is to be perpetually in his presence, "vulnerable" to it, as one of our younger monk priests likes to say in his Sunday homilies.

Inevitably, there are moments when fidelity to this presence does entail suffering. Just this morning, I read in Rilke's poem "In the Drawing Room" a comparison between the elegant courtiers of the seventeenth and eighteenth centuries and us:

> They [the courtiers] wanted to bloom
> And to bloom is to be beautiful.
> But we want to ripen,
> And for that we open ourselves to darkness and travail.

Darkness and travail are inseparable from the long middle time, "dry but nourishing." They are necessary for the passage from green to gold to brown. As Meister Eckhart wrote, "When a man scrapes the rust from a vessel, the vessel feels no pain. But when God scrapes the rust from us, we feel it, because the instrument is working on living flesh." Darkness and travail are intense moments of growth when the heat and light of Christ are most insistently penetrating our being. For most of us, they are the exception, rather than the rule. The long movement from seedtime to harvest is in general quiet. But however it may be, we "remain in the light," as the apostle John says, because we know that ripeness is all.

Chapter Thirty-Four.
Looking in a New Direction

The week after my solemn profession, an elderly monk of the community asked me to be his spiritual director. Thus began a wonderful friendship of weekly visits to the infirmary to speak with him over the course of ten years—until I left the United States and came to Brazil. Our meetings were always "Direction Plus"—sometimes he showed me photos of his Scotch-Irish forebears (I remember one photo that featured his dad in uniform for his work on the Canadian railroad), sometimes he recounted adventurous moments of his past, sometimes he broke out a small stock of candy (*all* monks like candy), sometimes he asked my opinion on a point of theology.

Of the hundreds of conversations we had, the one I most remember was when he asked me if my most frequent thought was the desire for heaven. I blushed, at least inwardly, because I believed that as a monk heaven was the place to which my thoughts should habitually revert. Although embarrassed, I answered truthfully, explaining that I wished that I could say yes, but I couldn't. He laughed, and said that at my age he couldn't have said so either. "Well then, how did it happen?" I asked him. "Was there a particular, recognizable moment, or was it just something gradual that you became aware of after it had taken place?" "As a matter of fact," he said, "there *was* a particular moment. One day I was praying, or reading, or just thinking—I'm not sure which—and suddenly I felt a hand on my neck, and someone twisting it. All of a sudden I was facing in another direction. Up until then, I always looked at *this* world. Even if I looked at the future, it was a question of wanting something in this world or being afraid about something that might happen in this world. But ever since that experience, my gaze is on the future. I can see heaven in the distance, and I want it. It's not that I try to think about heaven. It's just that I'm always longing for it." "How old were you, Father, when it happened?" "Somewhere around sixty."

I tucked that conversation into my memory, and I don't think it has ever left me. Some conversations you never forget. In this case, I don't just mean that it was always available for recall, that I could summon it up on my inner screen at will. I mean something more than that. In some way, the conversation continued being broadcasted live in me, Father George's testimony to the possibility of truly having one's heart fixed on God and eternal life. Two words above all echoed in me over the years: *heaven* and *sixty*.

One thing that gave me grounds for hope was that Father George and I were like two peas in a pod. He wasn't the classical saintly monk, and I wasn't the classical saintly monk. He had something of the curmudgeon in him, and I had the rest of it in me. He was very sensitive, and I was very sensitive. So it seemed to me that like the yearning for heaven, this "seeking the things that are above," the "desire to be dissolved and to be with Christ," the "inward dwelling in heaven" (*Conversatio nostra in coelis est*)—all of these phrases citations from the great Saint Paul—could possibly be the destiny, the portion, not just of the extraordinary monk, but of every monk. It might represent a natural step in the monk's organic evolution. The only way to find out would be to make a point of surviving until the age of "somewhere around sixty."

This I have succeeded in doing. As I write this chapter, I am on the verge of turning sixty-nine. There are tremendous benefits to this: I get to take the tramway on the Pão de Açucar (Sugarloaf Mountain) in Rio for half price; I get to board the airplane ahead of the customers classified as Gold, Sapphire, and Diamond. People are starting to get up and give me their seat on public transportation. But far and away the best of all, the very best of all, is that someone (Someone) has twisted my neck as well, perhaps not so thoroughly as in the case of Fr. George, perhaps not in such a clearly defined moment. Nonetheless, I am looking in another direction. My old conversation partner of the infirmary, long departed to the home he so ardently desired during the last thirty years of his life, must be interceding for me.

What is it like, you ask, to have a permanently twisted neck? It might sound painful to someone who has not gone through the experience, but actually, it is a relief. In the first place, the unrealistic dreams of accomplishment cease. You simply and peacefully know that you are not going to produce anything surprisingly glorious. The decent, honest work that you have done until now—what you have been doing and got used to doing— you will keep on producing. You needn't worry about giving birth to a *War and Peace* or a Ninth Symphony or a Michelangelo Pietà. If that baby hasn't been born by the time you're sixty, then you're not the one who's going to give birth to it.

The same is true on the moral level. If you have had to fight with impatience or melancholy or consumerism until now and have not yet succeeded in transcending them, then rest assured: they will be companions of the journey until the end. Self-knowledge and prayer will slowly diminish them, slowly smooth out their contours, slowly make you more careful not to hurt other people's feelings with your personal frailties. Still and all, your weaknesses are here to stay, for just the same time as you are here to stay.

And on the spiritual level as well. Somewhere around sixty, the monk (along with many others, I'm sure) will have the experience of standing at the end of his life's journey, of seeing his whole life as a completed whole, as finished, as past. In this experience there will be nothing to look forward to, in human terms; everything will be seen as over and done with. This makes possible a peaceful, objective evaluation of the whole sweep of one's life. Peaceful, objective, and *humbling*—for the monk sees how truly imperfect and poor his fidelity has been, how much less than what Christ had invited him to, how much less correspondence to grace there has been than he had fondly imagined for so many years. The great Portuguese Jesuit preacher of the seventeenth century, Antônio Vieira, often said that one of the most important tasks in life is "to die before you die" (Second Sermon for Ash Wednesday). Perhaps he meant that in terms of freedom from attachment. I suspect, however, that he meant it in terms of an anticipated Last Judgment. It is strangely wonderful to look one's fundamental poverty in the eye, unflinchingly, and to accept it, because it is the truth. "God is not fooled," Saint Paul said in one of his sterner moments. It is a great blessing not to need to fool oneself either anymore. I know about me what God knows about me. We have no secrets from each other.

As the delusions melt away, the genuine wonders appear. Other people, without changing a bit, take on a new dignity and beauty in our eyes, once our neck has been twisted (new for us, because in God's eyes they always had this dignity and beauty). Of late I have been catching myself looking at my contemporaries—monks, nuns, and assorted others—and being wonderstruck by their loveliness and goodness. Their silver hair, white hair, no hair (and all the rest of the catalogue) could be the basis for a new Canticle of Canticles. Certainly they can't be described as "running like gazelles," but there *is* a beauty there, physical and interior, that deserves to be celebrated in poetry. And there is something infinitely moving about their virtues, their determination to love, which has survived every temptation and even every fall.

And heaven? Heaven, of course, is God. All the theologians and mystics know that. When you hit sixty and God's age is eternity plus sixty (the sum of your age and his age), God comes out of the forest. God steps out from his hiding place in the trees. God lifts his adorable head out of the water and shakes the drops away. He lets himself be felt in the evening between the walls of your room, and betrays his presence in the wild cry of a flying duck. In the original text of the Song of Songs, the Bridegroom says, "You have wounded my heart, my sister, my love." In this new Canticle for senior citizens, we sing to God, "You have twisted my neck, my Father, my God, my Lord, my Love." Now that I look on you, I long to be where you are. It is not hard to have your desire fixed on heaven once God has made you glimpse it.

Chapter Thirty-Five.
The Beautiful Old Man

We are blessed in having a good number of other monasteries in the nearby states of São Paulo and Minas Gerais, and blessed in the fact that frequently monks or nuns from these communities come to visit us for a day, make a retreat, or participate in a liturgy of monastic profession. At some point during their stay, they invariably ask the question, "Do you know what we envy about your community?" "What?" "Your elders. We have lots of young people in our communities, but it would be really wonderful to have a few elders, people who have persevered in the life for fifty or sixty years and been transformed by it."

This appreciation of the preciousness of the elder has been a constant in the monastic tradition, right from the days of the Egyptian desert. If today's secular cultures idolizes youth, monastic culture has always had a spontaneous and profound veneration for age. Obviously, not simply for the accumulation of years, but for the product of decades of refining and polishing on God's part and of fidelity and openness to the work of the Spirit on the monk's part. The end product—the monk at the home stretch of his earthly race—is something quietly stunning. Like a sunset that turns the clouds purple and orange and rose.

As a matter of fact, it is precisely the category of beauty that monasticism has always employed to describe the unique quality of an aged monk. From the fourth century onwards, he has been known as the *geron kalos*, the beautiful old man. Certainly the monks of antiquity knew that they were playing with a paradox: that in the mind of most people, beauty is the special province of the young, a commodity that progressively decreases with time, so much so that there is not much difference between the withering of the very old and the ugliness of death. The desert monks were not insensible to the beauty of youth; indeed there are some marvelous anecdotes about the capacity of the elderly monk to glorify God for the beauty of an attractive young woman encountered on the road to or from Alexandria where the monks went to sell the baskets they wove to make their living.

At the same time, the desert monks found themselves before a startling and undeniable phenomenon: there exists another kind of beauty that consists in the transfiguration of the physical by the spiritual. The spirit shines forth in the flesh of these elderly monks and nuns. Their bodies are like delicate alabaster vases, and the life of the Spirit within them is like an oil lamp perpetually kept alit. The result is that these ancients simply glow; the Spirit has made them lastingly luminous. Our Cistercian Father Isaac of Stella writes in his *Fifth Sermon for the Feast of All Saints* (5.7) that in the joint residence of flesh and spirit that is the human condition, we will inevitably go in one of two directions. Either the Spirit in his divine liberty will work so successfully within our human liberty that we will end up with our whole self spiritualized, body included (this isn't Manichaeism but simply an anticipation of eternal life), or the impulses of the flesh will come to dominate us so completely—our thoughts and attitudes as well as our actions and words—that even our inward spiritual self will become materialized, carnalized.

The beautiful elder is the story of the victory of two liberties in perfect harmony with one another: the liberty of the Holy Spirit and our human liberty. In this *geron kalos*, we get a glimpse of the "spiritual body" that Saint Paul says we will all have when Christ returns and raises us up to glory; in fact, in the holy elder, we experience one of the most convincing proofs of the resurrection. It is there before our eyes. We see and touch immortal life.

It would be an interesting experiment to write a panegyric on the beautiful elder, to praise his loveliness from head to toe, with many intermediate stops along the way. In the scope of this chapter, however, we will satisfy ourselves with a very quick tour, pausing only at those places that have received a five-star rating.

Without any doubt, the most beautiful feature of the elder is his *smile*. It is absolutely open and spontaneous. It is not kept in check by shyness, it is not twisted by cynicism, it is not "hollywoodized" by a consciousness of being before the camera of other people's opinions, it is not cheapened by containing some hidden request, as if the monk wished to buy your benevolence with a smile and then ask you for a handout. The smile of the beautiful old man is simply there. When you find him, you find it. You are not the principal source of it—don't flatter yourself into thinking that. It springs from his happiness in God; it springs from his delight in God, who has made his dwelling in him. Yet, at the same time, the smile *is* meant for you, *is* produced by you. The peaceful happiness that he stably experiences simply by living and by living in the presence of God is reenergized by your appearing on the scene.

That is what explains one of the loveliest details in monastic history, mentioned earlier in the book, but worthy of being repeated: how the great nineteenth-century Orthodox monk, Saint Seraphim of Sarov, greeted each of the thousands of visitors who came to his cell for a blessing, confession, or spiritual direction with the salutation, "Welcome, my joy." Saint Bernard writes that we only truly love our neighbor when we love him in God, when we love him within our all-inclusive love for God. When a person reaches this state, then every human being is one more manifestation of God. That is why the elder's smile glows a bit more brightly when he catches sight of you.

Speaking of catching sight of: along with the way the elder smiles, what is most extraordinary about him is the way he *looks* at you. All of us are familiar with the saying that "the eyes are the mirror of the soul." Whether we want to or not, we inevitably reveal ourselves through our eyes. We reveal what it is we have been looking at as well as the response it has drawn forth from us—acceptance or rejection, lust to possess or yearning to give, condemnation or compassion, bitterness or sweetness. Jesus talks about having an eye that is single. By this I think he means an eye that is still, calm, focused, unwavering, accustomed to looking at God.

The gaze of an elder is penetrating without being judgmental. It looks into your depths, but without curiosity; it is not "fishing for old boots and tires in your inner lake," as a former spiritual director once expressed it. It is not at all inquisitive: it simply does what an eye is meant to do—it sees. But even more important than seeing, it communicates, and what it communicates is its own light. Jesus says, "The eye is the lamp of the body," and the elder's eye is a lamp not only for his own body but for yours as well. When he looks at you, your mood improves. Your hopefulness increases. Your perception of the tremendous good in people and things (whether latent or manifest) is liberated. What is happening? By merely looking at you, the elder is infusing his vision of reality into your heart. This is not hypnotism or brain-washing. As Saint Paul says, "For now we see in a mirror, dimly." But the elder has come very close to seeing things as they really are. His gaze makes it possible for you to look upon the real—at least for as long as your encounter with him lasts. And something of that encounter remains in you and changes you lastingly for the good.

Finally, there is his *touch*. We all remember our mother's touch and think that no one can ever touch us again with the same tenderness, the same affection, the same commitment, the same purity. But our mother's touch is itself a sacrament of the touch of God, and that sacrament can be relived in the touch of an elder. The touch of a true elder is always a blessing, whether he is tracing the sign of the cross on our forehead or imparting a quick hug when we are about to set off on a trip. It is a creative contact, like the touch of God the Father in Michelangelo's *Creation of Man*, where at God's touch Adam springs into life. It is maternal and Marian as well: there is always a hint of the presence of Our Lady in the embrace of an elder. It is not at all sentimental, or fussy. Rather, it is invigorating and strengthening, like the sacrament of confirmation. If all this has made you want to know our elders, come to visit us and see them for yourselves. But you can't have them! They are God's gift to our community.

Chapter Thirty-Six.
Death and the Far Side of Death

Death comes in threes, the saying goes. To conclude this series of reflections on "The Making of a Monk," I would like to describe three artistic monastic deaths—and what lies beyond them. The first death is portrayed in drawings, the second through literature, and the third in the genre of a dream. All of them have the same intuition about the reality and the ultimate significance of the death of a monk.

Perhaps you know the charming book of Mother Geneviève Gallois, OSB, *The Life of Little Saint Placid*. Published originally in 1953, it is a picture book with captions, the imagined life of an ordinary good Benedictine monk ("Everymonk") recounted in approximately one hundred pen and ink drawings. According to one version of the story, Mother Geneviève was asked by a novice to draw a picture for her for her feast day. Mother Geneviève, who had been an artist before entering the convent, got carried away and ended up composing a complete monastic biography in cartoons. When we first meet little Placid, he is a child oblate, entrusted by his parents to be raised by the monks and become one of them. The book follows his career—his aspirations, his experiences, his moments of temptation, his victories over them through grace and the love of the Virgin.

There are many extremely striking images in the collection, but the most moving of all are the final diptych. The next-to-last image shows Placid lying on his bier. He is terribly, hatefully dead. (Baldwin of Forde, twelfth-century English Cistercian father, says in his *Tractate on the Love of God* that these are the terms that most accurately describe death: *terribilis* and *odibilis*.) Although he is shown in repose, holding a crucifix and his vow formula between his folded hands, he is repugnant: shrunken, skeletal, vacant, totally dis-animated. The reader who has found himself irresistibly drawn into friendship with the vibrant little monk in the course of reading the book feels horror and sorrow at his final ugliness. Mother Geneviève wants us to know that this is how death is. It is not perfumed, it is not romantic, it is not sublime. It is what Saint Paul says it is—the last enemy—and apparently an enemy that has triumphed.

Then we turn the page (in our first reading of the book we may not even know there still is another page), and we discover to our joy the final plate of the series. Placid is young again; Placid is dancing in his work habit, his heavy work clogs light on his feet. He is being guided in an elegant *pas de deux* by an angel, and we know where the dance is leading because of the brief text that enfolds the dancers: *In Paradisum deducant te angeli.* "May the angels lead you into Paradise." This prayer, which makes up part of the liturgy of the Requiem Mass, we see being answered by God. Placid is there before us, being led by a wide-eyed and broadly smiling angel into the Father's house. That is the flip-side of death, the far side of death. Communion, beauty, joy.

You may also, perhaps, be acquainted with the second of these three monastic deaths. It is taken from the last great novel of Dostoyevsky, *The Brothers Karamazov.* The youngest of the brothers, Alyosha, is for much of the book a novice in a Russian Orthodox monastery. After Christ, the great light of his life is his spiritual director, the elder Zossima. Zossima is a controversial figure: people come from immense distances to consult him and to ask for his prayers and his blessing, but within the monastery itself, he is considered by many a source of annoyance and disturbance to the monastery's tranquility, if not a downright charlatan. For Alyosha, however, there is no doubt: Zossima is a living saint. He is the wisdom and uprightness and gentleness of Christ available to the novice whenever he wishes to seek him out in his cell.

Zossima is an elder, both in the charismatic sense and in the chronological sense, and a few hundred pages into the novel Zossima dies. By this point, we the readers are just as infatuated with Zossima as Alyosha is. Dostoyevsky has truly succeeded in incarnating in this fictional character the ideal of Eastern Christian monastic holiness. Alyosha is naturally saddened at his elder's death, but he sees in it the opportunity God needed to reveal Zossima's perfection and to glorify him publicly. Certainly miracles will begin to take place right at the time of the burial; certainly an aroma of roses will emanate from the body of the elder; certainly it will be next to impossible to prevent people from trying to obtain first-class relics of the saint.

These ardent expectations of the novice make what actually happens almost unbearable to him. Instead of roses, the stench of decay sets in almost immediately, in even less than the normal span of time. Instead of miracles at the gravesite, it is necessary to advance the time of the funeral and get it all over with as quickly as possible because, to put it plainly, the corpse stinks. Zossima's enemies in the community are jubilant. God has indeed spoken, and he has left no doubt that Zossima was nothing but a fake.

But Zossima is not a fake. He is simply a dead monk who has willingly (Dostoyevsky seems to imply an element of choice on Zossima's part) entered into the inevitable destiny of all mortals. Our body is "sown in corruption . . . is sown in dishonor . . . is sown in weakness . . . is sown as something merely physical" (1 Cor 15:42-44). That is what dying is about. It is not about roses and miracles and relics. It is our supreme poverty. Zossima wants Alyosha to know that, to know that about *him*—there are no exceptions—and Dostoyevsky wants us to know it about ourselves.

But here too there is one more page to the story. Months later, when Alyosha has let go of his futile hopes, he has a dream of Zossima. Zossima and he are mysteriously together, along with the Lord, at the marriage feast of Cana, and the wine and joy of eternal life flow in abundance. Zossima is feasting, and Zossima is serving, and Alyosha upon waking recognizes that Zossima did not come to an end at his grave. He passed into death, and he passed through it. For having been sown in corruption, dishonor, weakness, mere physicality, he has been raised "imperishable . . . glorious . . . powerful . . . spiritual." No wonder that Dostoyevsky took as the epigraph to his masterpiece the words of John 12:24: "Unless a grain of wheat falls into the ground and dies, it remains alone; but if it dies, it bears much fruit."

Finally, a third death. This one you cannot know, because I dreamed it the day before yesterday. In my dream, I had just received a package of books from Amazon (our monk accountant can tell you that this a more frequent occurrence than you may think). Two of the three books had been damaged in transit, which displeased me. I reached for the third book, hoping to find it in better condition. It was in fact in perfect condition, but it was completely black. The front cover and the back cover and all the intermediate pages of thick construction paper were black, with nothing written on any of them. It was the book of my death; I am sure of it.

Stuck in the middle of the book, however, emerging from between two pages, was a long white envelope. No address was written on it; nor was there any indication of the sender. As far as I know there was not a sheet of paper within the envelope. But the important thing, the crucial thing, is that it *was* an envelope. And in the dream I knew it was an envelope to and not from. At the moment of my death the envelope could be trusted to guarantee that the book would reach its destination. And the book's destination? As poor and dark and mysterious and incomprehensible as the book was, its destination was God, is God. Of that I am completely sure as well.